Bedworth and the Great War

Trevor Harkin

2009

War Memorial Park Publications

Bedworth and the Great War

First Edition 2009

Published by War Memorial Park Publications

ISBN: 978-0-9563727-1-0

For a copy of this publication e-mail trevorharkin@btinternet.com

Cover features Sappers James Swain and an unknown colleague in a photographic studio. Copyright Garry Woollaston

In Honoured Memory of the

Bedworth Men

who fell and served during

The Great War

Contents

Preface

Having researched my own family tree, in 2005 I began a project to research the memorial plaques in Coventry's War Memorial Park. The plaques commemorating those who died in the Great War and Second World War gave few details about the individuals purely initials, surname, rank and regiment. This interest in local history and those who fought in the Great War grew as I received more information via a web page, www.warmemorialpark.co.uk.

Several years later, 'Bablake School and the Great War' was published, followed by 'War Memorial Park'. 'Bablake School and the Second World War', 'City of Coventry : Roll of the Fallen. The Second World War' and finally 'City of Coventry : Roll of the Fallen. The Great War'. Following an exhibition; 'Kiss Ethel For Me' by the Bedworth Parsonage Centre based on the letters of Private Thomas Harrison I became intrigued by the men who fell and served from Bedworth. This is my sixth book and covers the men who fell and served from Bedworth during the Great War.

Trevor Harkin

Acknowledgments

Researching and compiling this book would not have been possible without the support of my wife, Emma and children Molly and Toby allowing me to indulge in this passion. The Commonwealth War Grave Commission (CWGC) Head Office who were fundamental in helping with the complex searches and background information, in particular Maureen Annetts and the Leamington Spa Office for information on grave location in the UK.

Researching the content of this book would have been impossible without the assistance of Vince Taylor and John Burton from the Bedworth Parsonage Centre who provided insight into Bedworth and Jim Nicholson, Secretary of the Bedworth Armistice Day Parade Group for permission to use images and content.

The records maintained by Coventry Heritage and Arts Trust and Bedworth Library and Information Centre have been essential in adding information to the details of the fallen and those who served, and their permission to use pictures and photographs is gratefully acknowledged. The following also need thanks; Terry Patchett for access to Bablake School archives, David Baynham from the Royal Warwickshire Museum, Kevan Darby for information on the 9th Battalion, Royal Warwickshire Regiment, Alan Tucker, Royal Warwickshire Regiment Database, users of the Great War Forum, Steve Morse, Author of 9th (Service) Battalion Sherwood Foresters (Notts & Derbys Regiment) during The First World War, Diane Fisher for access to the index of local papers in Coventry, Lee Lindon for information on Private Samuel Reynolds, Roydon Buckler for access to the medals of Private Amos Twigger and Lance Corporal Thomas Marston and Neil Clark for information on Second Lieutenant Tom Freeman.

The assistance of the following relatives of those who fell and served is gratefully acknowledged Vince Haughey (Private Alfred Martin), Garry Woollaston (Sapper James Swain) and permission to use an image for the cover and Damien Kimberley (Private Reuben Kimberley).

The Evidence

Throughout this book various resources have been compiled to build a database of the men who served and those that fell from Bedworth. Materials from the Coventry Heritage and Arts Trust and Bedworth Library and Information Centre were fundamental for underpinning this project. The principal document used was the 'Our Boys' book completed after the war by the 'Our Boys' Committee, sub-sections of the booklet covered *'Fallen Heroes'*, *'Prisoners of War'* and *'Men who served with Colours'*. The names inscribed on the Bedworth War Memorial were also a piece of key evidence.

Other sources have been consulted: *'Soldiers who died in the Great War'* with the search criteria of enlisted, resided or born in Bedworth. The *'City of Coventry: Roll of the Fallen'* compiled in 1927, includes the names of 2,600 men who fell and were either born, employed or resided in Coventry. Detail on each entry varies but typically covers name, rank, regiment, former regiment, address, birth details, occupation and in some cases employer. A small number of Bedworth men were covered in this Roll.

The Commonwealth War Graves Commission were kind enough to provide a list of all casualties with Bedworth in the next of kin details. Details were also obtained of any registered Commonwealth War Grave burial in Bedworth Cemetery.

Local papers have been consulted, *'The Coventry Graphic'*, *'Midland Daily Telegraph'*, *'Nuneaton Observer'*, *'Bedworth and Foleshill News'* and *'The Coventry Herald'*. For those who attended Bablake School or have plaques in Coventry's War Memorial Park or had a connection to Coventry my previous books have been consulted.

The National Archives of Australia in particular the Mapping Our Anzacs Project and the Library and Archives of Canada with the Soldiers of the First World War database. Information obtained during research has been shared with these bodies.

In some cases the *'Battalion War Diaries'* have been acquired, although generally they only name individuals if they were Commissioned Officers. Privates and Non-Commissioned Officers were generally not mentioned; the diaries` entries vary in length dependent on the operations that day. In some cases the date wounds were received has been verified, in the remainder the action the Battalion was involved in on the day or just prior to the date has been included.

If further details can be supplied please contact me on 07762511234 or via the website www.warmemorialpark.co.uk. The pictures used have in the majority of cases been digitised from microfilche and therefore the quality is variable.

It is important to note, however, that the cross- referencing of material has raised anomalies, in particular order of forenames, middle names, rank, spelling, address, etc. In these cases I have gone with the majority. Anomalies also occurred with the date of death. *'The London Gazette'* provided citations and announcements of promotions although some difficulties were encountered with the search criteria. Original records should be consulted if clarification or further information is required.

Bedworth: A Brief Introduction

Bedworth is a market town in the Nuneaton and Bedworth district of Warwickshire and is situated five miles north of Coventry and three miles south of Nuneaton. Evidence of the town dates back to the Doomsday book of 1086. The five miles from Coventry is an important part of Bedworth's history, the introduction of the 1665 Five Mile Act forbade any assembly of non-conformist church goers for worship and preaching within five miles of a town such as Coventry, Bedworth town centre for this reason was set just outside of this limit. At the turn of the century the town had a population of approximately 11,000 inhabitants, today the town has an estimated population of 42,000 mainly due to it's transport links to neighbouring cities. Originally a small Saxon market town, the opening of the Coventry Canal in 1769 and later the railway in 1850 enhanced the town's growth. In the 18th and 19th centuries, Bedworth developed into an industrial town due largely to coal mining and the introduction of ribbon weaving and textile industries from nearby Coventry.

Records show that coal had been extracted from Bedworth and the surrounding area since the 13th Century. The opening of the Coventry to Bedworth canal in 1769 stimulated output and subsequent canal construction made Warwickshire coal competitive in London. Rapid railway development in the 19th century increased demand still further and deeper mines were exploited. Prior to the outbreak of the Great War, thirty pits were outputting over 4,000,000 tons, a substantial increase from the 500,000 tons from 20 mines in the 1850's.

In the 18th century in addition to the mining industry, Bedworth had a thriving and prosperous silk ribbon industry. This highly skilled work was brought to the town by the French Protestant families, the Huguenots, they set up hand-looms in their own homes and taught their craft to the locals. The Cobden treaty of 1860 with France removed the duty on French silks entering England and led to the collapse of the ribbon weaving industry. Although some ribbon weavers emigrated, those that stayed earned a living carrying out decorative bead crochet work which was very popular during the later part of the Victorian era.

After the collapse of the ribbon trade, the arrival of hat making (a tradition to the neighbouring towns of Nuneaton and Atherstone) aided Bedworth's growth; this industry lasted until the mid 1950s. The close links with Coventry meant that workers were attracted to the car factories in Coventry and away from the traditional mine work after the Second World War. Newdigate Colliery ceased production in 1982 and the neighbouring Coventry Pit was closed in 1994.

The boundaries of the town have altered over time, in 1894 Bedworth was a civil parish within the Foleshill Rural District. In 1928 Bedworth was incorporated as an urban district in its own right and finally in 1974 the Bedworth Urban District was merged with the borough of Nuneaton to create the borough of Nuneaton and Bedworth.

Bedworth and the Great War

In 1914, Europe was a divided and complicated place. Britain and France were suspicious of Germany which was building up a large navy; Britain had a powerful navy whilst her ally France complemented this with a huge army. Russia also had a huge army and as the Russian royal family, the Romanovs, was related to the British Royal Family the trio of countries hoped to persuade Germany not to provoke trouble in Europe.

At the turn of the century, Britain owned a quarter of the world and was experiencing economic success. In an attempt to counteract this Germany colonised territory in South Africa. With a disagreement on navy sizes, South Africa and neighbouring countries in Europe being divided, the political scene only needed one incident to spark off a conflict, this incident occurred at Sarajevo on the 28th June, 1914. The heir to the Austrian Empire, Franz Ferdinand, was visiting Sarajevo, and was shot along with his wife by a member of the Black Hand Gang, Gavrilo Princip. The gang wanted to rid Bosnia of Austrian rule and to unite Serbia with Bosnia to form a new Balkan state. Austria blamed Serbia for supporting the Black Hand Gang and planned to invade, Serbia planned to ask Russia for help. Austria then called on Germany for help, the German government agreed and their response provoked the French government.

Prior to the assassination, Germany had been working on her own plan, termed the Schlieffen Plan; this calculated that the Germany Army could invade Belgium and France, beat them within six weeks and then attack Russia. A 1839 treaty guaranteed that if anyone attacked Belgium, Britain would come to her defence. On August 4th 1914, Germany invaded Belgium. Britain declared war on Germany, with France and Russia supporting. Austria declared support for Germany and so the Great War began.

The initial effect on Bedworth was minor, the *'Bedworth and Foleshill News'* covered the Bank Holiday sports day of the 3rd August, 1914: "*An entry of 150 was received and the handicapping done so that some remarkable finishes resulted. The programme comprised three flat events and two cycle handicaps and an air gun competition. The attendance was disappointing, the meagre character of the crowd being due to 'counter-attractions' and the fact that many parishioners were away on holiday*".

Another issue of local importance was noted in the *'Bedworth Old Meeting Church Magazine'*, the Reverend J. F. Bradley wrote with reference to Police and prosecution : "*There is an uneasy feeling creeping over the public mind that our policemen are becoming practised trap setters a doubtless necessary to catch lunatics....We are not sentimentally pleading for leniency for the wilful law breaker we are pleading that policeman are allowed discretion and where possible a warning precedes the summons.*"

On the 7th August, 1914 *'The Coventry Herald'* under the headline, *'The True Cause of War'* analysed the outbreak and declaration of war: "*The catastrophe which has hung over Europe for more than a generation has fallen on the innocent and telling people of all countries with a sudden and stupendous swiftness. For years the European Continent was formed into an armed camp. Great and little nations prepared for the day, and the dark cloud which is hanging over Europe at the present time may not be lifted for many a day. Britain provoked by the aggressiveness of the Prussian military spirit, has been drawn into the vortex of fire and blood...The Strategy of smashing France without delay and then be free to attack Russia...that scheme has failed.* "

As the war continued, so did affairs in Bedworth. October, 1914 saw the announcement of the death of Mr. Edwin . J. Beal a highly respected inhabitant of Bedworth aged 73. His obituary stated, "*He had come to Bedworth many years ago as licensee of the King's Head Hotel a position in which he retired in 1910, when his son Harry succeeded him. He was a native of Sudbury. For forty years or so he was a close friend of Mr W. Johnson MP. He was an enthusiastic sportsman and a great supporter of Bedworth Town Cricket club.*"

On the 2nd November, 1914 the local paper noted: "*Among the members of Bedworth Church Institute who have joined the colours are Messrs. A. Haywood (assistant secretary), R. Lovett, F. Dewis, J. Allen, F. Carter and H. Russell. The Institute send presents to all the above and Mr. A. Newman accepted the office vacated by Mr. Haywood.*" Arthur Haywood of the Grenadier Guards, son of Mr. John Haywood of Roadway Bedworth was later given a commission in the 12th Royal Warwickshire Regiment.

In December 1914, '*The Coventry Herald*' announced '*The platform at Bedworth Train Station will be raised and afterwards paved, it is evident from this that the townspeople will have to be thankful for small mercies*'. On the 4th December, 1914 it was noted for Holidays – It is expected that the shopkeepers of Bedworth will observe only Christmas Day and Boxing Day as holidays.

At the start of the following year under the headline: '*Bedworth Answers The Call*' it was reported that Bedworth had a highly successful meeting in the Girls Central School with the emphasis of providing further stimulus to recruiting in the mining town. With a list of dignitaries attending, Mr. Wm. Johnson MP sent his apologies as he was unable to attend due to his connection with the West Yorkshire Miners dispute. However he noted that 53 men had enlisted since Christmas. Also unable to attend but due to military duties was Captain Sir William Wiseman serving with the Duke of Cornwall's Light Infantry. His letter quoted the story of a young man who stated if the country was invaded by Germans he would go and fight, the Captain replied: "*It would be too late by then to do any good.*"

Canon Evans officiating the meeting declared in his opinion "*this was one of most important meetings that had ever been held in Bedworth*", he was treated to a round of applause when he concluded, "*almost to spend our last pound and our last man before we give in.*"

As the war progressed, '*The Nuneaton Observer*' dated 21st May, 1915 reported that the only German living in Nuneaton was taken from his home in Abbey Green to Warwick by Detective Horseman to be interned, no reference was made to any Germans being residents of

Bedworth. In 'The Bedworth and Foleshill News' dated 19th June, 1915 the following advert appeared (the recruiter Colonel Wyley based in Coventry was to lose his only son in the war).

7th BATT.

ROYAL WARWICKSHIRE REGIMENT.

(3rd. LINE DEPOT).

500

RECRUITS WANTED AT ONCE

FOR IMPERIAL SERVICE.

APPLY:

THE BARRACKS, COVENTRY.

W. F. WYLEY. Colonel.

'The Bedworth and Foleshill News' in July, 1915 covered the burial of two Bedworth men who had been killed in the Exhall Colliery disaster which had taken numerous lives in July, 1915. The first was William Jackson, aged 17, from 92, Bulkington Road and the second burial an hour later was Ernest George Noel Marsden aged 27. At a memorial service at Bedworth Parish Church, Canon F. R. Evans pointed out that some of the rescued men even went back to help comrades and this had

18

cost the lives of at least one of the miners, "*and although they did not get VC's, their work was equally commendable*".

In 1915 James Swain, aged 28, enlisted with the Royal Engineers as a Sapper. He was born on the 7th October, 1887 at Bull Ring Terrace, Chilvers Coton and arrived in France on the 9th November, 1915 with the 8th Entrenching Battalion. Just over a month later on the 15th December, 1915 he joined the 175th Tunnelling Company and was gassed which necessitated a return to England until the 21st March, 1916. On arrival back in France he worked primarily in the Ypres Salient area at Railway Wood engaged in tunnelling and mining with the 177th Tunnelling Compay. During 1917/18 he was engaged in the Somme/Cambrai areas repairing roads, bridges and other activities. He was demobilised on the 10th February, 1919 and returned to his occupation as a coal miner. James died at the age of 68, in Bedworth on the 30th July, 1956.

Sapper James Swain

19

The death of a banksman and haulier, Joseph Fletcher was reported on the 22nd October, 1915. Aged 60, he was driving across the railway sidings at the Charity Colliery, Bedworth where he had gone to obtain coal. The jury who investigated concluded that the normal rules of shunting had been applied and a warning given.

Better news was reported by *'The Midland Daily Telegraph'* on the 3rd December, 1915: *"Elisabeth West aged 13 who is leaving the George Street Council School, Bedworth this week has never been absent for over nine years. She entered the school on May 14th, 1906. Her sister, Norah who left the school in July 1914 had a similar record. Even more remarkable is the fact that there are seven younger children in the same family."*

Throughout Britain the Government had introduced a Military Service Act on the 2nd March, 1916, as Lord Derby's Scheme had failed to provide sufficient recruits. The first act called for compulsory enlistment of unmarried men of between 18 and 41, exemptions would be granted on the basis of occupation, hardship, faith or moral belief. Each exemption request would be heard by a local tribunal and the outcome of tribunals at Bedworth were covered in the local papers.

On August 3rd, 1916 the Bedworth Military Tribunal dealt with thirteen claims for exemption. Amongst the appeals were men who were willing to return to colliery work from other occupations, however the tribunal pointed out that *'600 men were in Warwickshire pits now who weren't there when the war started'*, The tribunal refused these applications.

On September 9th ,1916 the *'Bedworth and Foleshill News'* covered the 'Appeal Tribunal' of Alfred Twigger. He was employed by his father as farmer and dairyman, his father applied for absolute exemption as he had sacrificed two sons and had no-one to take this one's place. He was granted 25 days exemption.

The Chairman of the Tribunal took the time to note: *"Among today's appeals were a considerable number of newly employed munitions workers whose appeals had been dismissed by the tribunal. The chairman said if they grant exemption in such cases they would have everyone running to them to escape service. They must first get permission or there was no use in running to them".* The tribunals held seem to have been objective and consideration was given to farmers appealing for exemption for workers during harvest or those that faced the collapse of businesses.

The Reverend J. F. Bradley in the March 1917 issue of the *'Bedworth Old Meeting Church Magazine'*, suggested *"that the line must be drawn at suggesting that all bad munitions timekeepers had to be sent to the front. Why not send the overeaters, over drinkers and over gamblers."* The outcome of 'Tribunals' was still an emotive subject in the latter days of the war and in May 1918 W. H. Smith of Heath Road, Bedworth felt compelled to write to the *'Bedworth and Foleshill News'* on the subject of *'Butchers exemptions'*: *'Why should the miners who have been working six or seven shifts per week to help the country be send to the front at a few days notice while tradesmen working two or three shifts per week are left behind to overcharge the relatives the miners are leaving behind'.*

'The Coventry Graphic' on the 30th June, 1916 showed two scenes relating to Bedworth, the first a garden party at Sindon House, the residence of Mr. and Mrs. T. Topp with the objective of the party was raising funds for the Primitive Methodist Church new building scheme. The second scene was a life boat flag day in aid of the National Life Boat Institution: a *'goodly sum'* was apparently collected.

Garden Party at Bedworth.

Coventry Graphic Photo.

A garden party held at Swindon House, Bedworth, the residence of Mr. and Mrs. T. Topp, with the laudable object of raising funds for the Primitive Methodist Church new building scheme.

Life-boat Flag-Day at Bedworth.

The news of September 23rd 1916 focussed on a fire on a goods train going from Nuneaton to Coventry when it pulled into Bedworth. A quick thinking railwayman disconnected the offending carriage and with residents and by means of rope rescued the fair ride gondolas that were aboard. Additionally a £1,000 organ was saved, it was noted that no train services were delayed.

The Bedworth Voluntary Protection Committee were continuing operations in October 1917, and a meeting of the protection committee with Mr. John Daffern presiding discussed any necessary steps in the case of air raids. Superintendent Drakeley commended the team on the steps taken for last year but warned about possible air raids during the coming winter. Arrangements were made for patrol and other duties with gaps being filled where necessary.

On a national level *'The London Gazette'* on the 30th March, 1918 published details on the liquidation of the   EXHALL WAGON COMPANY Limited.

NOTICE is hereby given, pursuant to section 188 of the Companies (Consolidation) Act, 1908, that a Meeting of the creditors of the above named Company will be held at Exhall Colliery, Bedworth near Nuneaton, on Friday, the 12th day of April/1918. at 2.30 o'clock in the afternoon,.— 032 ARTHUR BIRKITT, Liquidator.

Pictured Mr. Daffern and others at the opening ceremony and the gun and some of the spectators

Just prior to the end of the war, *'The Coventry Graphic'* on the 8th November, 1918 reported that it was *'Bedworth's Week'* to *'Feed the Guns'*. With the paper reporting; *"The effort had its inauguration on Monday when a procession through the principal thoroughfares aroused considerable interest. Those taking part included members of the Parish Council and prominent residents, land girls, school children and a gun loaned by the War Office. The campaign was formerly opened in the Market Square by*

23

Mr John Daffern, Chairman of the Parish Council and the speakers included Canon Evans and the Reverend J. F. Bradley. An unfortunate accident befell a youth named Cyril Dickson of Collycroft who was run over by one of the wheels of the gun carriage sustaining shocking injuries. After receiving attention he was removed to the Coventry and Warwickshire Hospital".

The following week, *'The Coventry Graphic'* reported the death of Mr. John Randle who died in his 92nd year; *"The deceased was a sidesman at the parish and the most wonderful man in Bedworth. His wife died in 1916 after a married life of 68 years".* The same edition covered the belated award of the Edward Medal to a Mr. John Johnson. The award was given for bravery and devotion on the occasion of an accident at the Newdigate Colliery in July, 1915.

A heavy fall of roof occurred and a deputy named Joseph Pacey was buried. In making an attempt to assist the imprisoned man, Johnson was also buried and eventually the two men were liberated and removed to hospital. Pacey died and Johnson did not recover completely from his injuries. He received the medal from the King at Buckingham Palace. In February, 1919 he was awarded £100 from the Carnegie Heroes Fund. It is thought that the belated honour was bestowed due to the anxiety arising out of the war at the time of the incident.

February, 1919 saw Mr. John Daffern, Chairman of Bedworth Parish Council resume his public engagements after a serious illness. At the Parish Meeting, Mr. W. H. Alexander congratulated Mr. Daffern on his recovery. The Chairman announced *"He was much obliged. It has been the longest and most severe illness, I have ever had".* During the war, Mr. Daffern had led a number of committees and sub-committees in efforts relating to the war.

In April, 1919 a handsome reredos was placed in Bedworth Parish Church in memory of Mrs. Wootton of Southfields, Longford and her eldest son, Mr. Harry Wootton. The reredos sculptured in alabaster with side panels of carved oak was described as a 'magnificent piece of work'. The inscription reads: *This reredos was erected to the Glory of God and in loving memory of Emma Rebecca, beloved wife of Edward Wootton, who departed this life January, 19th 1918: also of Charles Henry (Harry) Wootton who died October 16th, 1918.*

The 19th July, 1919 was set aside by the Government as Peace Day. The Peace Celebrations Committee had been formed in advance and notes made in June, 1919 by the Hon. Secretary (Mr. T. Topp) that an anonymous parishioner had donated £14 in prizes in connection with a procession. A discussion pursued at the Committee by Mr, W. H. Alexander and the Reverend W. O. Pugh and the Reverend J. F. Bradley who tried to ascertain if some schools had an unfair advantages knowing that characters were expected on the floats. Judges were decided upon and the prizes allocated as £2, £1 and twelve of 10/-each with twenty prizes of 5/- each. The procession began at Marston's Lane at 1.00pm.

Our Boys Fund

At the end of the Great War a souvenir booklet was issued by the 'Our Boys' Fund this has been replicated in the following pages and supplemented with related articles. The fund was set up to assist the families and the men who had enlisted from Bedworth. The Appendix lists the Prisoners of War and those who served with the Colours.

Preface

In October, 1915 at the invitation of Mr. W. Johnson Jun. a meeting was held at the Miner's Office, at which a Representative Committee was formed with a view to raising a fund for the purpose of providing Christmas parcels for all those men serving in HM Forces who had enlisted from Bedworth.

The matter was taken up with enthusiasm, a ready and generous response was made to an appeal for subscriptions and Christmas parcels were duly sent to all the men thus eligible. As the War continued it was found desirable to enlarge the scope of the Fund, so as to enable the Committee to award Christmas Gifts each year to the dependents of the men who had fallen, and to send parcels of food to the Bedworth prisoners of war. To meet the ever increasing demands for all these purposes, more money was required and various methods of raising the necessary amount were devised. These included house to house canvassing, a flag day, auction sales, concerts, sales of work, church collections, cinema shows, draws, whist drives and a football match.

All of these were generously supported, the total amount raised on behalf of the fund being £1,700. In the later years of the War the gifts to the men serving took the form of money, as being safer in transmission and more appreciated by 'Our Boys'. The gratitude of the recipients has from time to time been expressed in hundreds of letters and postcards forwarded to the secretaries, and the discharged soldiers and sailors have since testified through their representative, Mr. A. H. Lawrence, their appreciation of the work of the Committee, of the generosity of the subscribers, and of the impartial manner in which the fund has been administered.

The Committee also desires to thank all who have in any way contributed or helped. This souvenir containing the names (with Regiment, Honours etc) of every Bedworth man who has served in the Navy, Army or Air Force during the War, is presented to each one and to the nearest dependents of the Fallen, in slight, but grateful recognition of all they have done in service of King and Country. All honour to them and to their brave Comrades who have made the Great Sacrifice.

'*The Coventry Graphic*' dated 14th September, 1917 under the headline '*Remarkable Auction Sale at Bedworth*' reported on the successful effort for the 'Our Boys' Fund with a miscellaneous auction sale. The event took place on the grounds adjacent to the residence of Mr. G. Pickering, J. P. *Nearly 500 lots were offered ranging from a bullock to a bottle of ink. Never before had such a heterogeneous collection been offered at Bedworth and needless to remark the sale aroused the greatest interest. The 'entries' embraced in addition to the articles mentioned, about twenty fat lambs, several pigs, numerous couples of fowls, ducks, rabbits, a horse, loads of coal and firewood, furniture, garden implements, household requisites, cigars, wine, spirits, beer and stout, grocery, wearing apparel etc. Messrs Courtaulds very generously gave a number of silk scarves, silk blouses, sports coats, crepe-de-chine blouses, dress lengths etc.* Pictured are Alderman W. Johnson M. P., in the preliminary proceedings connected with the formal opening of the sale, some of the officials and the auctioneers.

Opening of the Sale

The following month on October 6th 1917 it was reported in *'The Coventry Graphic'* that the fund had realized a sum of £37 to augment a fund for Christmas comforts; proceeds then stood at £132 and it was hoped they would rise to £500. Sale of sheep raised funds to £186. Alderman Johnson had received various letters from France and illustrated them with the following example; *"I am writing to congratulate your members of the funds. I am sure all boys here from Bedworth are more then pleased at the way Bedworth people are working to help with the world's great struggle."* Signed 1592, Bombardier Jack Sherratt.

In May, 1918 an 'Our Boys' meeting held at the Parish Room, showed the balance sheet. The fund had raised about £543 but the Christmas comforts had taken this down to £30. Emphasis was increased as further efforts were required to meet costs due to increasing numbers of prisoners. After the end of the war and with Christmas 1918 approaching the Committee decided on the 23rd November, 1918 that a Christmas gift of 10s to every man who enlisted from Bedworth would be made and it was decided to distribute gifts to widows and children and dependents of the Fallen. Mr W. H. Alexander presided over this meeting.

Bedworth Men in the News

After the outbreak of war, it was quickly announced that men would be needed and appeals were placed in the local papers, locally 600 men were identified for the Royal Warwickshire Regiment in a campaign led by Colonel Wyley. By December 1914 it was reported that the Bedworth recruits who enlisted in Lord Kitcheners Army had left for the front although not all the local men found themselves in the Royal Warwickshire Regiment. News from the front appeared in all the local papers.

The *'Bedworth and Foleshill News'*, 3rd April, 1915 provided updates on two Bedworth youths. *Alec McDonagh son of William McDonagh of Nuneaton joined the regular forces in August, 1914 being attached to the Coldstream Guards. His father and four uncles went through the Boer War and he also has a brother serving somewhere in France. He has been four months in the trenches and distinguished himself gaining the rank of Sergeant. He was home for a short time having been invalided and returned to the front*

 The other update was on Private Herbert Kidger of the Worcesters, who was in hospital in Rouen suffering from gunshot wounds to the left thigh. Private Kidger was brought up by Mr. E. H. Parsons of the Post Office, Bedworth. Writing to Mr. Parsons the wounded man said *"I was wounded on 12th March, 1915 but I am getting along alright."*

In May, 1915 *'The Coventry Graphic'* printed two *'Local Rolls of Honour'* for Bedworth men with the colours. The first printed on the 7th May, 1915 included photos of forty two men whilst the second publication showed a further seventy men.

Bedworth Men with the Colours (1)

1. *Private H. Sharpe, 4th Bn., Royal Warwicks 2.Private S. Sharpe, 9th Royal Warwicks 3. Private F. Sharpe, 9th Bn., Royal Warwicks 4. Sergeant B. Sharpe, 3rd Bn., Royal Warwicks 5. Private W. Sharpe, 1st Bn., Royal Warwicks 6. P. J. Lole, Royal Field Artillery 7. F. W. Lole, Royal Field Artillery 8. Private W. Lee, Oxford and Bucks 9.Private J. Golby, Oxford and Bucks 10. Private Golby, Royal Warwicks 11. Private A. Golby, 6th Dorsets 12. Private H. Wight, Royal Warwicks 13. A. Evans, Royal Field Artillery 14. Private Brown, Grenadier Guards 15. Private C. Ward, Royal Warwicks 16. Private E. Blount, 3rd Leicesters 17. Private Neale, Royal Warwicks 18. J. Neale, Royal Horse Artillery 19. Lance Corporal A. Marriott, Royal Warwicks 20. Private H. Hill, Royal Warwicks 21. Private J. Frogatt, Royal Engineers 22. Private W. J. Hopkins, Royal Warwicks 23. Private W. Timms, Oxford and Bucks 24. Private W. Jackson, Royal Warwicks 25. Private C. Lucas, Royal Warwicks 26. Private C. Farley, Royal Warwicks 27. Private J. Gazey, Royal Warwicks 28. Private E. V. Wright, Oxford and Bucks 29. Private H. Sproson, Royal Warwicks 30. Private H. Harris, 9th Lancers 31. Private Poole, Royal Warwicks 32. H. Harris, Royal Garrison Artillery 33. Private J. Orton, Royal Warwicks 34. Private H. Wright, Northamptonshire Regiment 35. J. Farndon, Royal Field Artillery 36. Private J. Dalton, Lancashire Regiment 37. J. Mockford, Royal Field Artillery 38. Private G. Dyall, Royal Warwicks 39. J. Smith, Royal Field Artillery 40. Private F. Allen, Royal Warwicks 41. Private W. Goode, Oxford and Bucks 42. Private D. Wood, Royal Warwicks*

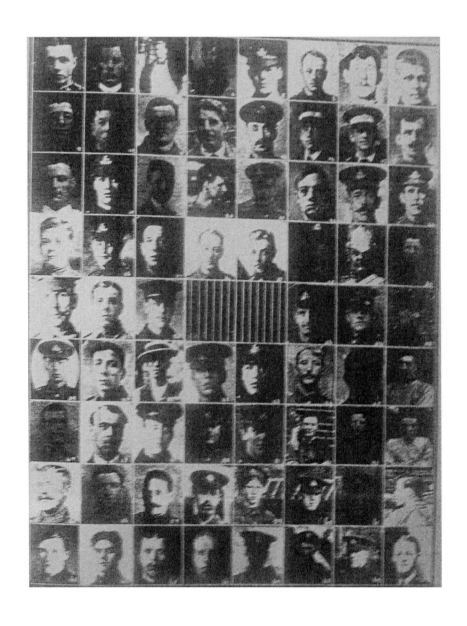

Bedworth Men with the Colours (2)

1. Private A. Hopewell, 2nd Royal Warwicks 2. Private J. Adams, 2nd Welsh Regiment (Missing) 3. Private J. Twigger, Army Service Corps 4. Private J. Harvey, 11th Hussars 5. Private J. Ludford, Oxford and Bucks 6. Private N. Randle, Royal Warwicks 7. Private M. Treadwell, Coldstream Guards 8. Private Mainwaring, Royal Warwicks 9. Sergeant F. Wright, Royal Field Artillery 10. J. Wright, Royal Horse Artillery 11. T. Cave, Royal Garrison Artillery 12. Private Campion, King's Own Yorks Light Infantry 13. F. Prideaux 14. A. Whitehall, St. John's Ambulance 15. E. Whitehall, St. John's Ambulance 16. Private T. Wilshee, Royal Warwicks 17. Private Willett, 1st Leicesters 18. Private Oulton, 3rd Royal Warwicks 19. Private T. Harrison, 7th Royal Warwicks 20. Private A. Harrison, 2nd Royal Warwicks 21. Private J. Paddy, Royal Warwicks 22. Private F. Sherwood, Canadian Contingent 23. Private C. Plumridge, Royal Warwicks 24.Sergeant Whitehouse, Royal Field Artillery 25. Private Tibbitts, Oxford and Bucks 26. Private A. E. Hunt, Royal Warwicks 27. Private Hunt, 2nd Royal Warwicks 28. Private E.Armitage, Royal Warwicks 29. G. Phillips, 1st Life Guards 30. Private Fallis, Oxford and Bucks 31. Private Foley, Royal Warwicks 32. Private Gudger, Oxford and Bucks 33. Rifleman F. Brown, King's Royal Rifles 34. Private N. Randle, Royal Warwicks 35. Private J. Randle, Royal Warwicks 36. Private H. Marple, Royal Warwicks 37. Sapper Poole, Royal Engineers 38. J. T. Cornish, Royal Field Artillery 39. J. Crutchlow, Royal Warwicks 40. Private S. Ford, Royal Warwicks 41. Private A Ford, Oxford and Bucks 42. Private J. Ford, Wiltshire Regiment 43. Private S. Rowlands, Royal Warwicks 44. Private Darlison, Grenadier Guards 45. Private J. Hill, Royal Warwicks 46. Private J. Coughton, Oxford and Bucks 47. Private F. Robinson, Coldstream Guards 48. Private J. Long, Royal Warwicks 49. Private J. Hogden 50. G. Ludgate, Oxford and Bucks 51. Private H. Ludgate, Oxford and Bucks 52. Private G. Wagstaffe, Oxford and Bucks 53. Private J. Nicklin, Oxford and Bucks 54. Private T. Tidman, Oxford and Bucks 55. Private J. Edwards, 6th Worcesters 56. Private Leslie Lee 57. Private J. Davis, Army Service Corps 58. Private J. Bradshaw, Duke of Cornwall's Light Infantry 59. Private J. Taylor 60. Private H. Palmer 61. Private F. Palmer 62. Private S. Henton, Royal Warwicks 63. Private D. Aucott 64. Private J. Tedds, Royal Warwicks 65. Private J. Blundred, 2nd Royal Warwicks 66. Private W. Blundred, 3rd Royal Warwicks 67. Private W. Smith, Royal Warwicks 68. Private G. Taylor, Duke of Cornwall's Light Infantry 69. Private J. Pittam 70. Private P. W. Hunt, Duke of Cornwall's Light Infantry

33

The *'Bedworth and Foleshill News'* the following month featured Sergeant John Davenport Johnson, the third son of Alderman Wm. Johnson M. P of Dovedale, Bedworth, who was in his final year with the Warwickshire Yeomanry when war broke out but enlisted for a further period of service. Before going to Egypt he guarded German prisoners at Newbury racecourse. It was noted that some of his colleagues were killed during the torpedoing of the Wayfarer.

'The Coventry Graphic' on the 11th June, 1915 printed a picture of : A number of miners from Bedworth district who are training to go to the front to combat the effects of gas-poison among the troops with the headline 'Gas Fighters for the Front'.

Gas Fighters

'*The Nuneaton Observer*' reported a member of the 7th Battalion, of the Warwickshire Territorial Force, Private T. Bucknall, had been awarded the Distinguished Conduct Medal. Bucknall whose home was at Bedworth attracted attention by his daring rescue work in a mine gallery near Fricourt at Tambour Du Court on 21st August, 1915. The gallery was foul with gas and in total darkness he welcomed the opportunity of going to the rescue of some of his colleagues of the Royal Engineers, Tunnelling Company.

Other detail was added by rival newspapers; "*Just 20 years of age, Private Tom Bucknall enlisted in the 7th Warwickshire Regiment a few days after the outbreak of war. Being a collier and the son of a collier, and therefore inured to the danger of mining operations he subsequently became attached to the 174th Tunnelling Company of the Royal Engineers. He attended Bulkington Infants School and his name appears in the school Roll of Honour. Curiously enough the teacher who taught Private Bucknall at that school expressed the hope in a recent letter to the young soldier, that he would be able to win some military honour. Prior to joining the Army, Private Bucknall was employed at the Newdigate Colliery. His home was at Navigation Terrace, Bedworth and his father employed by the Criff Colliery. The young soldier was a regular attendee at the Bedworth General Baptist Chapel, and he secured several prizes. Private Bucknall formerly played football for a Bulkington Association team.*"

On the 26th September, 1915, Corporal Walter Leonard Shortridge, 43279, earned his DCM at the age of 25. His citation stated: "*for conspicuous gallantry near Hulluck, when he laid a telephone wire under heavy fire, and remained on the end of it for half an hour in the open in the rear of the gun trench until ordered to withdraw. He showed great coolness bravery and devotion to duty.*" Walter was the son of Councillor Shortridge of Coventry Road, Bedworth. He left the Central Schools at the age of 13, entering Bablake School where he stayed for three years leaving in 1906. Walter's education was furthered at Coventry Technical College and at

35

Birmingham. He enlisted on the 1st September, 1914 as a sapper being stationed in Ireland for a while before going to France in August, 1915 and promoted to Corporal in the 16th Signal Company, Royal Engineers. Notification of his Military Medal was published in *'The London Gazette'* on the 4th February, 1918.

'The Coventry Graphic', 19th November, 1915 under the headline' Bedworth Man Severely Wounded' ; ' A remarkable escape from death has been experienced by Private Sidney Farndon of 112, Bulkington Lane, Bedworth who is recovering from wounds at Falmouth Hospital. Private Farndon enlisted in the 2nd Royal Warwicks, after the outbreak of war, and in recent action came under a withering fire. He received six shrapnel wounds in the left side, three bullet wounds in the left arm and a bullet wound in the temple and was picked up in a serious condition. Before the war Private Farndon was a miner at Exhall Colliery.

The Battle of the Somme saw reports appearing in the *'Bedworth and Foleshill News'.* On the 22nd July a stirring account was provided by Bedworth man H. Ken Bosworth who wrote to his former employers, K. Wooton and Co. describing the scene. *"I have been up the line for ten days, seeing things, and dodging shrapnel, whizz-bangs etc. By God, It's something to be able to say you have been through present day action and come out safely. To come down here for a few days is peaceful. It's a God-send to be away from the roars of the guns for a while.*

Last Saturday morning was a sight never to be erased from one's memory to see the boys come out of the trenches and steadily go over to the Germans' line. From our dressing station we could see them go over. It was not long before we had to turn out and make the regimental aid posts and bring down the wounded, and we were tied on all that day and Sunday. During Saturday it was not safe to bring the fellows over the top. All the cases had to be carried down the trenches as the doses of shrapnel were arriving too quickly.

We did climb out once to see if it was safe, and a shell burst a few yards away. We ducked and quickly too. The Germans had the Aid Post well in line for they were pitching shells round almost all of the day. Two of the regimental stretcher bearers were killed at the entrance of the dug-out from where we collected and that was the sight we saw when we first went up – not very encouraging I can tell you.

The sights to be witnessed in the trenches of the dead were horrible to be touched upon in a letter. Although there was a large number of wounded, I think the percentage of dead was slight in comparison with other engagements. Our artillery had done some excellent work. The ground had simply been ploughed up. I can only say there must be a lot of Germans, buried there, so their losses can at the best only be estimated. Two of the worst days I spent were in the village we captured. God! It was terrible. The Germans of course knew the exact positions of the roads, and they were aware we should be using them for bringing out fresh troops, ammunition etc. and didn't they send some shells over! Still with it all, I am safe and sound for which I'm truly thankful."

The following week, 29th July, 1916 it was reported *"Private Benjamin Davis son of Mr. George Davis is currently at a Military Hospital in Edinburgh he was struck by shrapnel fire in the knee early in the great advance. Also wounded Private A. Griffen 22777, Royal Worcesters."*

Two Bedworth men were reported as wounded on the 23rd September, 1916 with the Royal Warwicks Private T. A. Bull, 5442 and with the Northamptonshire Regiment, Private J. Williams, 17609. Another report from the 11th November, 1916 covered wounds to Private W. Kendell, 16850, Oxford and Bucks and with the South Staffordshire, Private J. Burns, 17078.

'The Nuneaton Observer' and *'The Coventry Graphic'* in May, 1917 covered the severe wounds of Second Lieutenant Pickering. *'The Nuneaton Observer'* under the headline *'Bedworth Officer Wounds'* stated *'Second Lieutenant S. G. Pickering, Royal Warwickshire Regiment who has been so severely wounded that it has been necessary to amputate his right leg above the knee, he is the only son of Mr. G. Pickering, Chairman of the local Bedworth Tribunal. In a letter to Mr. Pickering, Lieutenant W. J. Croft says "It was*

really remarkable your son ever got back at all. He was wounded within twenty yards of the enemy lines and it was after the larger part of the men had retired. His servant stood by him nobly and actually dragged him back to our lines whilst there was the usual hell of lead flying about".

'*The Coventry Graphic*' reported on the 29th June, 1917 that Private F. G. Jackson of the Royal Warwickshire Regiment was sometime ago reported as missing and his parents had come to the conclusion that he was killed. He did however send better news stating that he was alive in a prisoner of war camp in Germany. The following month came the award of the Military Medal was to Sergeant Isaac Randle.

On the 30th October and the 2nd November, 1917 came notification of the awards of Military Medals to Gunner Fred. A. Bosworth, 840636, and Bombardier Joseph Farndon, 840657 both were in the Royal Field Artillery.

'*The Coventry Graphic*' on the 2nd November, 1917 under the headline '*Gassed and Wounded*' reported that Private H. Burbury (of Collycroft), 1st Royal Warwickshire had been gassed and wounded in France.

'*The Coventry Graphic*', under the headline, '*A Former Bedworth Pastor*' on the 7th June, 1918 reported that "*News has reached Bedworth of the death at the front of Lieutenant-Colonel the Reverend Donald Fraser DSO, the chaplain of the forces who some years ago was a Free Church minister at Bedworth. His death was due to an accident. He was returning by motor from the morning church parade, when the car in which he was travelling was caught between two lorries and the Reverend was thrown out and died later. The deceased was mentioned in dispatches in 1916, and last year received the DSO. He went to Tamworth from Bedworth and occupied a seat on the Board of Guardians at the former place.*" The Commonwealth War Grave Commission provide further details, he was aged 42, and the son of Alexander Fraser of Auchgate, Cannich, Beauly, Inverness and is buried in Plot A. 2. Couin New British Cemetery, France and died on the 2nd

June, 1918. On the 12th July, 1918 Corporal W. Lownds, 207816, Royal Engineers was gazetted with the award of a Military Medal.

 In December, 1918 the *'Bedworth and Foleshill News'* covered the award of the Croix de Guerre with silver star by the French government for good work done during the evacuation of Arras in March, 1917 to Corporal J. B. Dunkley, 24 King Street, Bedworth.

Notification of Military Medals were published in *'The London Gazette'* in 1919. On the 21st January, 1919 came Gunner Thomas Bucknall, 117179, 291st Siege Battery, followed by Sergeant John Leach, 4424, 14th Bn., Royal Warwickshire Regiment on the 24th January, 1919 and finally Private John Whyman, 9711, 15th Bn., Royal Warwickshire Regiment on the 7th February, 1919. In October 1919, *'The London Gazette'* stated that Captain William Henry Carding MC relinquished his commission on the account of ill health with the 1st Res. Bn., South Africans but retained the rank of Captain.

Died at Home

Thirteen men are classified by the Commonwealth War Grave Commission (CWGC) as died at home, this means they are buried at locations throughout the UK. Nine men are buried in Bedworth Cemetery. A map showing the grave locations within Bedworth Cemetery can be found in the Appendix. Bombardier Bartlett is commemorated on a screen wall in Tottenham Cemetery, Private Lole is buried in Rothley Cemetery, Private Penn is buried in Norton (All Saints) Churchyard and Corporal Robinson is buried in Coventry's London Road Cemetery.

The first burial in Bedworth Cemetery was **Private George Conway**, 13080, Royal Warwickshire Regiment who died at home on the 14th July, 1915. George was born in Leicester in 1891 to Elijah and Kate Conway. He resided with his wife Selina Conway in Bedworth and enlisted in Nuneaton. Inscription reads: *'Our love is as dear today as in the hour he passed away'.*

The next burial was **Private Victor Reginald Parsons**, TR7/1085, 92nd Bn., Training Reserve and 17th Bn., Royal Warwickshire Regiment who died of sickness on the 30th May, 1917 aged 17. Victor was the son of Mrs. Ellen Parsons, of 15, Rosemary Villas, Collycroft, Bedworth. He was born in Leamington and enlisted in Coventry. Victor's name is recorded in 'Fallen Heroes' and on the Bedworth War Memorial.

The following month, **Private Thomas Henry Bowns**, 266446, 7th Bn., Royal Warwickshire Regiment died of wounds received in action on the 5th July, 1917 aged 19. A resident of Bedworth he enlisted in Coventry and his name appears in the 'Fallen Heroes' and on the Bedworth War Memorial. He has a private headstone which also relates some family information: *'Sacred to the memory of our beloved parents, Ernest Leonard Marshall Died 5th February 1965 Aged 67 and Getrude May Marshall Died 21st November 1969 also Thomas Henry Bowns Her brother who died of wounds July 5th 1917 Aged 19'*.

Four Bedworth men died at home during 1918. The first was **Private Henry Marples**, 33112, Somerset Light Infantry who died at home on the 20th February, 1918. He was one of the Bedworth Soldiers that appeared in *'The Coventry Graphic'* in May, 1915 and his name is recorded in 'Fallen Heroes' and the Bedworth War Memorial.

Driver Walter Harvey, 109788, Royal Field Artillery died at home on the 2nd April, 1918. He was aged 29 and married to Bertha Harvey (nee Chamberlain) of 16, Butler's Yard, High Street, Bedworth. Walter enlisted in Coventry, and his name is recorded in 'Fallen Heroes' although this document implies an association with the Northumberland Fusiliers.

Acting Corporal William A Tallis, 2018, 1st /6th Bn., Highland Light Infantry died as a result of wounds received in action at home on the 5th October, 1918 aged 31. William was the son of William and Mary Tallis and resided at 4, Cow and Hare Yard, Bedworth with his wife, Jessie Wallace Gray Tallis. His name is recorded in 'Fallen Heroes' and on the Bedworth War Memorial with his inscription reading *'He died that we might live'*.

October also saw the death of **Air Mechanic 3rd Class Ernest. R. F. Parsons,** 146684, Royal Air Force died at home on the 21st October, 1918. Ernest's name is recorded in both 'Fallen Heroes' and on the Bedworth War Memorial, 'Fallen Heroes' also refers to a A. M. Parsons with the A. M. standing for Air Mechanic.

Two soldiers were buried in 1919. The first was **Private Harry Page,** 16143, Hampshire Regiment who died at home on the 21st January 1919, aged 49. Harry was the husband of Ann Page, of 7, Spitalfields, Bedworth and his name is recorded on the Bedworth War Memorial.

Sapper George. W. Berrill, 43244, Royal Engineers died at home on the 23rd September 1919, aged 25. George was the son of G. W. and Florence Berrill, of 83, Wootton Street, Bedworth and is named on the Bedworth War Memorial.

The first soldier who died at home and was buried outside the boundaries of Bedworth is **Bombardier William Bartlett**, 32575, 118th Bty., Royal Field Artillery who died of wounds, on the 8th June, 1915, aged 29. William was the son of Richard and Sarah Bartlett, of The Moat Farm, Bedworth although he was born in Sudborough, Northampton and enlisted in Coventry. William is one of 291 burials in the western side of Tottenham Cemetery, Middlesex. As his grave could not be individually marked a screen wall commemorates his burial.

42

Private Harry Lole, S/255766, Army Service Corps died at home, on the 26th January, 1917. A native of Bedworth, the family must have moved to Rothley, Leicestershire prior to the war as Harry enlisted in Leicester and is one of only two first world war burials in Rothley Cemetery. The other being Sapper Charles Sleath, Royal Engineers a resident of The Cedars, Rothley who died on the 5th June, 1918.

Private Harry Penn, 24671, 2/8th Bn., Royal Warwickshire Regiment died at home on the 17th February, 1918 and is buried right of the main path in Norton (All Saints) Churchyard, Northamptonshire. He was the son of George and Susan Penn, of Norton and aged 25. Harry's name is recorded in 'Fallen Heroes' and on the Bedworth War Memorial.

Finally buried in Coventry's (London Road) Cemetery is **Corporal William Robinson,** 10825 Royal Warwickshire Regiment, secondary unit Labour Corps transferred to CSM, 95401, Royal Berkshire Regiment. William died on the 25th May, 1919 aged 44. A native of Bedworth, he resided in Coventry and enlisted in Coventry in January, 1915. During William's service he was awarded the Meritorious Service Medal whilst with 160th Coy., Labour Corps, this was awarded if soldiers performed especially meritorious service in difficult circumstances and details of his award appeared in the 'London Gazette' on the 18th January, 1919.

The inscription on his headstone reads ' At Rest'. William worked at the Rudge Works and his obituary in the *'Rudge Record'*: "*Co. Sgt-Mjr. William Robinson (Polishing Shop) had over four years of war, first with the Royal Warwicks and later with the Royal Berks. Sometime ago he was badly gassed, and this set up cancer. He was in hospital for several months suffering great agony, and eventually as there was no hope of*

recovery, he asked to be sent home, and was discharged on 19th May, 1919. He died six days later on the 25th".

Williams Discharge Certificate

Died at Sea

Three Bedworth men would die at sea during the course of the war. One death was as a direct result of enemy action.

Able Seaman Richard Bert Lucas, SS/120, (RFR/PO/B/6081) was lost at sea on the 11th March, 1915 when HMS Bayano was torpedoed and sunk by submarine U- 27. Richard, aged 31, was the son of William and Sarah Lucas, of Eurek Villa, Park Road, Bedworth and resided with his wife, Beatrice Lucas and two children, at 30, Longford Road, Foleshill, Coventry.

At the beginning of the war, British passenger liners and merchant ships were requisitioned by the Admiralty for conversion to Armed Merchant Cruisers (AMC's). After conversion AMC's although now armed, lacked armour and were vulnerable to attack and were mainly used for lone patrols and escort duties. One of these, the Bayano at 5948 tons was built in 1913 by Elders and Fyffes, requisitioned on the 21st November, 1914 and commissioned on the 21st December, 1914 to make up the Navy's deficiency in cruiser numbers and form part of the 10th Cruiser Squadron. Bayano, M78, was fitted with 2 x 6 inch guns and had a top speed of 14 knots.

Bayono prior to conversion

45

On the 11ᵗʰ March, 1915 she was on the way to Liverpool from the Clyde and off the coast of Ireland when she was sunk by U27. She sank in under three minutes. As most of the men were asleep below, the loss of men was approximately 195 although 26 men survived. Able Seaman Lucas is commemorated on the Portsmouth Naval Memorial. U-27 under the command Captain Wegener had started her patrol on 25ᵗʰ February and returned home on the 17ᵗʰ March with a route via the north of Scotland.

The translated diary of the U-27 records *"05.00am (German time), March 11ᵗʰ 1915. Large dipped headlights, commercial steamer only for warship held. Attack driven. Nose torpedo meets steamer in the front third. Range of fire 2-300m, size of the steamer approximately 8000t, dipped the headlights, nationality unknown. Steamer sinks with nose first in approximately 10 minutes. Three boats with torch/flare fire."* Weather observations generally clear with some patches of drizzle/fine rain. On a further patrol in August 1915, Captain Wegener of U-27 was controversially killed in the Irish Sea, by the men of another armed British merchant ship, the Baralong.

On the 9ᵗʰ July, 1917 **Able Seaman Robert Jones**, J/34057, HMS Vanguard was killed by internal explosion of the vessel at Scapa Flow, aged 19. Robert was born in Bedworth to Mr. and Mrs. Griffith Jones, and the family later moved to Arley where they resided at 20, Gun Hill.

The loss of HMS *Vanguard* and over 800 men is believed to have been caused by an explosion in one of the two munitions magazines which served the amidships turrets. Although no formal cause for the cordite explosion was ever found by the Court of Inquiry it was probable that a fire in a neighbouring area smouldered away undetected long enough to heat the cordite stored at an adjoining bulkhead to dangerous levels, triggering an explosion. Eyewitness accounts of the incident described seeing a bright flash or flame, followed by two heavy explosions and then a third, smaller one.

The Court of Inquiry also considered the possibility of sabotage. On the basis of the spelling of his surname, (perceived to be German) they investigated and subsequently cleared a Coventry man, Assistant Paymaster Edward Leslie Pierson who also died in the explosion.

Admiral of the Fleet, Lord Beatty, wrote a letter to his wife, two days after the loss of HMS Vanguard, he stated: *"A terrible calamity has befallen us and one of my fine old battleships blew up at anchor at 11.30pm, Monday night – the poor old Vanguard with over 1,000 men on board, in 25 seconds it was all over...... It is an overwhelming blow and fairly stuns one to think about. One expects these things to happen when in the heat of battle, but when lying peacefully at anchor it is very much more terrible."* Those who perished in the disaster are commemorated on the Chatham, Portsmouth and Plymouth Memorials, Robert is one of seventy four crew members commemorated on the Plymouth Naval Memorial.

The final death at sea was **Stoker 1st Class David Crutchlow**, SS/111261, HMS Narborough, who was killed in action on the 12th January, 1918. HMS Narborough was one of two destroyers that ran aground in severe snowstorms, at South Ronaldsay, Orkney, there were no survivors from the crew of 93 men. The other destroyer HMS Opal lost 95 men and had one survivor, Able Seaman William Sissons. He managed to swim ashore and kept himself alive with shellfish and snow. Notes made by his rescuers provided the main input into the Inquiry on the sinking of the two destroyers.

About 9.30 p.m. on Saturday, 12th January, HMS Opal and Narbrough were in company Opal leading. There was a thick blizzard on at the time and a heavy following sea. Opal struck heavily about three times and shortly after slid into deep water. Almost immediately after striking Opal was pooped by the following sea which filled up her after part and carried away her funnels and mast. After sliding into deeper water her fore part broke off at the break of the forecastle and the remainder foundered in about a quarter of an hour from striking. When Opal who had been sounding with sounding machine, struck she blew three blasts on her siren which were answered by Narbrough. Narbrough appeared to pass Opal on the port quarter, strike heavily and heel well over. Nothing more of Narbrough was seen by the survivor. Able Seaman Sissons states that Captain and Sub-Lieutenant of Opal were on the bridge at the time of striking and after striking orders were given to abandon ship. He did not observe any boat manage to get away safely and states that the Carley Floats were launched but owing to sea no one could remain on them. He considers that men on deck before the midship gun-platform should have had some chance of saving themselves but can give no information as to anyone from Narbrough.

The Inquiry found that a court marshal was not necessary as *" it does not appear that any further evidence throwing light on the losses would be elucidated."* Orders were sent to the rest of the Grand Fleet with recommendations. The Pentland Skerries and Stroma lights are sufficient navigational aids for making the eastern entrance to the Firth, and if these lights cannot be seen no vessel should attempt to enter at night. It was thought that the installation of an intermittent light would not be sufficient to counterbalance the assistance it would give to enemy submarines, etc.

David Crutchlow is recorded in 'Fallen Heroes' and the Bedworth War Memorial and commemorated with his colleagues on the Portsmouth Memorial.

Egypt

In March 1915, the base of the Mediterranean Expeditionary Force was transferred to Alexandria, Egypt from Mudros and Alexandria became a camp with medical units and hospitals. After the Gallipoli campaign of 1915, Alexandria remained an important hospital centre covering later operations in Egypt and Palestine and the port was used by hospital ships and troop transports bringing reinforcements and carrying the sick and wounded out of the theatres of war. Chatby Military and War Memorial Cemetery was used for burials until April 1916, when a new cemetery was opened at Hadra as it was realised that the cemetery at Chatby would not be large enough. Most of the burials in these cemeteries were made from the Alexandria hospitals.

Two Bedworth men are buried in cemeteries in Egypt. Private George Thomas Jacques is buried in Alexandria (Chatby) Military and War Memorial Cemetery and Driver Ernest Edward Carvell is buried in Alexandria (Hadra) War Memorial Cemetery.

Private George Thomas Jacques, 19027, 4th Bn., Worcestershire Regiment died of wounds received in the Gallipoli Campaign on the 3rd October, 1915, aged 26. Although he was a native of Bedworth, he enlisted and resided in Nuneaton.

Driver Ernest Edward Carvell, T4/093274, Royal Army Service Corps. attd. 130th Field Ambulance, Royal Army Medical Corps died on the 9th December, 1918 aged 20. He was the son of Caleb and Louisa Carvell, of Bedworth Hill and his name is recorded on the Bedworth War Memorial.

Gallipoli

The eight month campaign in Gallipoli was fought in an attempt to force Turkey out of the war, to relieve the deadlock of the Western Front in France and Belgium, and to open a supply route to Russia through the Dardanelles and the Black Sea. The Allies landed on the peninsula on the 25th to 26th April 1915.

On the 6th August, further landings were made at Suvla, just north of Anzac, and the climax of the campaign came in early August when simultaneous assaults were launched on all three fronts. However, the difficult terrain and stiff Turkish resistance soon led to the stalemate of trench warfare. From the end of August, no further serious action was fought and the lines remained unchanged. The peninsula was successfully evacuated in December 1915 and early January 1916.

The environment and circumstances in Gallipoli dictated that only one man of the six men who died from Bedworth has a known grave, the remaining five men have no known grave and are commemorated on the Helles Memorial along with 21,000 of their colleagues.

Private Ernest Twigger, 10988, 9th Bn., Royal Warwickshire Regiment, died of wounds, in Gallipoli on the 5th August, 1915. He was born in Bedworth and resided at 22, John Street, Bedworth with his wife, Ada. Ernest enlisted in Nuneaton and his name is recorded in 'Fallen Heroes' and on the Bedworth War Memorial. On his death he was buried in Beach Cemetery which was used from the day of the landing at Anzac, almost until the evacuation. There are 391 servicemen of the First World War buried or commemorated in the cemetery.

 Two Bedworth men were killed in action on the 6th August, 1915 and both are commemorated on the Helles Memorial. The first is **Private John Edwards,** 17852, 4th Bn., Worcestershire Regiment. John was born in Blackheath, Staffordshire and enlisted in

Worcester. A resident of Bedworth, his name is recorded in 'Fallen Heroes' and the Bedworth War Memorial.

The second man was **Private Leonard Lovett,** 23032, 4th Bn., Worcestershire Regiment formerly Oxfordshire and Buckinghamshire Light Infantry. Leonard was aged 20 and the son of Fred and Ellen Frances Lovett of Ferndale, Rifle Range Road, Ashby de la Zouche. Leonard was born in Ashby de la Zouche and enlisted in Nuneaton, his name is recorded in 'Fallen Heroes' and on the Bedworth War Memorial.

The following day, **Private, Israel Sharpe**, 3217, 6th Bn., Royal Munster Fusiliers was killed in action, aged 35. Israel was born in Bedworth, although the family must have moved to Aston, Birmingham as his parents, Amelia and Rufus, resided at 22, Sycamore Road, Aston. Israel enlisted in Pentre, Glamorgan and is commemorated on Panel 185 to 190 on the Helles Memorial.

On the 18th August, 1915 **Private Tom Speding,** 10624, 5th Bn., Dorsetshire Regiment was listed as killed in action, aged 36. Tom was the son of Mary and Jonathan Speding of 8, Kirkland, Lamplugh, Workington and the husband of Hannah E. Spedding, of 4, Sleath's Yard, Bedworth. He was actually born in Ulverston, Lancashire and enlisted locally in Nuneaton. His name is recorded in both 'Fallen Heroes' and on the Bedworth War Memorial.

Sapper Frederick Beauclerc Fox, 46974, 85th Field Coy., Royal Engineers died of wounds received at Gallipoli on board the hospital ship, Nevasa on the 31st August, 1915. He was formerly a resident of 18, High Street, Bedworth and a native of Sleaford, Lincolnshire. Frederick enlisted in Nuneaton at the outbreak of war and was previously employed as a motor body maker His name is recorded in 'Fallen Heroes' and on the Bedworth War Memorial.

Germany

The majority of First World War Commonwealth war graves in Germany were moved into four permanent cemeteries after the war. However, a few graves could not be moved on religious grounds or for other reasons and they remain in their original locations in German military and civil cemeteries. Among the 113 graves at Worms (Hochheim Hill) Cemetery is **Private William Ernest Smith,** 11487, 50th Bn., Machine Gun Corps (Infantry) formerly 14787, Royal Warwickshire Regiment. William died as a prisoner of war, aged 46 on the 5th October, 1918. He was born in Souldern, Oxford, enlisted in Nuneaton and resided with his wife, Alice Elizabeth (nee Golly), at 66, Roadway, Bedworth.

His name is inscribed on a screen wall in Worms Cemetery and on the Bedworth War Memorial, his name is also recorded in 'Fallen Heroes'.

Greece

From the spring of 1915, the hospitals and convalescent depots established on the islands of Malta and Gozo dealt with over 135,000 sick and wounded, chiefly from the campaigns in Gallipoli and Salonika, although increased submarine activity in the Mediterranean meant that fewer hospital ships were sent to the island from May 1917. Five Bedworth men are either buried or commemorated in Greece, Private, Thomas Jacques is buried at Pieta Military Cemetery, three men are commemorated on the Doiran Memorial, Private William Matthew Skinner, Private John Fullylove along with Private Thomas Bucknall, and Lance Corporal James Bird is buried at Karasouli Military Cemetery.

There are 1,303 Commonwealth casualties of the First World War buried or commemorated at Pieta Military Cemetery one of whom is **Private Thomas Jacques**, 9309, 9th Bn., Royal Warwickshire Regiment, who died of wounds received in Gallipoli whilst being treated at a hospital in Greece on the 22nd October, 1915. Thomas was born in Collycroft, resided in Bedworth and enlisted in Warwick with the Royal Warwickshire Regiment. His name is recorded in 'Fallen Heroes' and the Bedworth War Memorial.

The Doiran Memorial stands roughly in the centre of the line occupied for two years by the Allies in Macedonia, but close to the western end, which was held by Commonwealth forces. It marks the scene of the fierce fighting of 1917-1918, which caused the majority of battle casualties. From October 1915 to the end of November 1918, the British Salonika Force suffered some 2,800 deaths in action, 1,400 from wounds and 4,200 from sickness. The action of the Commonwealth force was hampered throughout by widespread and unavoidable sickness and by continual diplomatic and personal differences with neutrals or Allies. On one front there was a wide malarial river valley and on the other, difficult mountain ranges, and many of the roads and railways it required had to be specially constructed.

The first death of a Bedworth man commemorated on the Doiran Memorial is **Private William Matthew Skinner,** 20296, 2nd Bn., Duke of Cornwall's Light Infantry formerly 4462, Royal Warwickshire Regiment who was killed in action on the 17th November, 1916, aged 25. William was the son of Mrs. Teresa Ford of Bedworth Hill, Nuneaton. He enlisted in Nuneaton and was born in and resided in Exhall; as such he is commemorated on the Exhall Memorial.

Six months later, on the 25th April, 1917 **Private John Fullylove,** 13872, 12th Bn., Royal Hampshire Regiment formerly 7740, Royal Warwickshire Regiment was killed in action, aged 41.

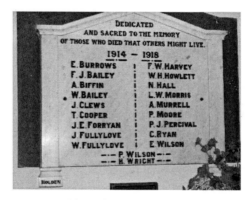

Chapel End Memorial

54

John a native of Ansley was married to Elizabeth Fullylove, of 28, Alfred Street, Gloucester although he resided at Hartshill and enlisted in Nuneaton. His name is recorded in 'Fallen Heroes', the Bedworth War Memorial and Chapel End Congregational Church.

John was one of four sons of Mr. Edward Fullylove of Old Oak House, Coppice Lane, Hartshill. It was reported in the *'Bedworth and Foleshill News'* under the headline, *'We are Seven'* that Edward was extremely proud of having four sons, two nephews and one son-in- law in the Army. Those pictured from top left to right are Private John Fullylove, (12th Hampshire Regiment), Private Walter Fullylove (Royal Warwicks), Private Arthur Fullylove (Royal Warwicks) and Private William Fullylove (King's Own Hussars). The son-in-law (the bottom row left) is Private William Ashby (Oxford and Bucks) and the nephews are Private Arthur Fullylove (Royal Warwicks) and Private Ernest Fullylove (Territorial's).

Commemorated on the Loos Memorial is a Private Walter Fullylove, 10527, 2nd Bn., Royal Warwickshire Regiment who died on the 25th September, 1915.

The final Bedworth man commemorated on the Doiran Memorial is **Private Thomas Bucknall,** 11353, 7th Bn., Oxfordshire and Buckinghamshire Light Infantry who was killed in action in Salonika on the 9th May, 1917, aged 37. Thomas was the son of Israel and Elizabeth Bucknall, of 18, Royal Oak Yard, Collycroft, Nuneaton, he was born in Bedworth and enlisted in Nuneaton. Thomas is honoured in 'Fallen Heroes' and on the Bedworth War Memorial.

Doiran Memorial

The final casualty in Greece is **Lance Corporal James Bird**, 15535, 7th Bn., Royal Berkshire Regiment who was killed in action in Salonika on the 13th March, 1917. James is buried in Karasouli Military Cemetery, which was begun in September 1916 for the use of casualty clearing stations on the Doiran front. The cemetery contains 1,421 burials of the First World War. James was born in High Broughton, Lancashire, enlisted in Coventry and was a resident of Bedworth.

India

 From the Bedworth men who fell there is one commemoration in India on the Kirkee Memorial. **Private Walter Griffin,** 12804, 9th Bn., Royal Warwickshire Regiment who died of wounds received in Mesopotamia, on the 9th May, 1916 aged 30 whilst fighting with the forces trying to relieve General Townshend. The Kirkee Memorial commemorates more than 1,800 servicemen who died in India during the First World War, who are buried in cemeteries in India and Pakistan where their graves can no longer be properly maintained. It also includes the names of 629 servicemen whose remains were brought from Bombay (Sewri) Cemetery for re-interment here in 1960. Walter's wife, Lillian Griffin, of 7, Chamberlain Street, Bedworth received notification that he husband died at Victoria Hospital in Bombay and his remains were possibly one of those men re-interned.

Walter was born in Bedworth to Thomas and Maria Griffin and enlisted in Ilkeston, Derby with the 7th Royal Warwicks he was previously a member of the militia and had seen active service. An employee of the Newdigate Colliery, he left a widow and seven children. Walter's name is recorded in 'Fallen Heroes' and on the Bedworth War Memorial.

Iran

On Armistice Day, 11th November, 1918 **Private James Reynolds**, 22991, 9th Bn., Royal Warwickshire Regiment died in Mesopotamia. He was born in Ryton and enlisted at Bedworth. Locally his name is commemorated in 'Fallen Heroes' and on the Bedworth War Memorial. Private Reynolds who lost his lives during the campaign in Iran (formerly known as Persia) has no known grave and is commemorated on the Tehran Memorial. This memorial is located in Tehran War Cemetery which is within the British Embassy compound at Gulhak and has 3,590 names inscribed.

Tehran Memorial

Italy

Four Bedworth men are either commemorated or buried at four different memorials or cemeteries in Italy. The Italians entered the war on the Allied side, declaring war on Austria, in May 1915. Commonwealth forces were at the Italian front between November 1917 and November 1918. In March 1918, three divisions relieved Italian troops on the front line between Asiago and Canove, the front being held by two divisions with one division in reserve. The French held the line to the left, with the Italians to the right. The front was comparatively quiet until the Austrians attacked in force in the Battle of Asiago which lasted one day from the 15th to the 16th June 1918. The Allied line was penetrated to a depth of about 1,000 metres on 15th June but the lost ground was retaken the next day. Between June and September, frequent successful raids were made on the Austrian trenches. In October, two divisions were sent to the Treviso area of the River Piave front. The Austrians were finally defeated in the Battle of Vittorio Veneto which lasted from the 24th October to the 4th November 1918.

There are five Commonwealth Graves on the Asiago Plateau and Bedworth men rest in three of these. Private Thomas Darlison is buried in Granezza British Cemetery, Private Thomas Dericott in Boscon British Cemetery. They both died on the 15th June, 1918. Private J. T. Edwards rests in Cavalletto British Cemetery, he died on the 16th June, 1918.

Private Thomas Darlison, 43872, 8th Bn., King's Own Yorkshire Light Infantry formerly 5/21859, 6th T.R. Battalion was killed in action and is one of 142 First World War burials at Granezza British Cemetery. The son of William and Elizabeth Darlison of Bedworth he was born in Bedworth, enlisted in Coventry and died aged 22. His name is recorded in 'Fallen Heroes' and on the Bedworth War Memorial.

Private Thomas Dericott, 11386, was also killed in action, with 1st /4th Bn., Oxfordshire and Buckinghamshire Light Infantry. He was aged 27 and the son of Harriett and Thomas Derricott. Thomas was born and resided in Bedworth although he enlisted in Nuneaton. He is one of 166 First World War servicemen buried or commemorated at Boscon British Cemetery, it is possible that his original burial was at a different location as a number of the graves were brought in from other cemeteries after the war. Thomas's name is recorded in 'Fallen Heroes' and on the Bedworth War Memorial.

'Fallen Heroes' records the name of Edwards, J. T. Royal Warwickshire Regiment. There is only one such recorded which is **Private John Thomas Edwards**, 34718, 1/6th Bn., Royal Warwickshire Regiment who was killed in action on the 16th June, 1918, age 31. He may have resided or enlisted in Bedworth as his parents Thomas and Esther Edwards resided at Runcorn, Cheshire. As John is buried at Cavalletto British Cemetery, it is likely he was treated at an advanced operating station where urgent cases from the front were dealt with. The journey from the mountains to the main hospitals was long and difficult so an advanced operating station was established.

The final soldier killed in action is **Private John Johnson**, 201959, 1st /5th Bn., Royal Warwickshire Regiment who fell in a raid near Coda, south-west of Asiago on the 9th September, 1918 aged 21. He has no known grave and is commemorated on the Giavera Memorial. John was the son of George and Elizabeth Johnson, he was born and resided in Bedworth and enlisted in Coventry. His name is recorded in 'Fallen Heroes' as Jack (a name also used for John's) and on the Bedworth War Memorial correctly as John.

Mesopotamia

During the First World War, in November 1914, Basra became the base of the Mesopotamian Expeditionary Force. Amara was occupied by the Mesopotamian Expeditionary Force on 3rd June 1915 and it immediately became a hospital centre. The accommodation for medical units on both banks of the Tigris was greatly increased during 1916 and in April 1917 seven general hospitals and some smaller units were stationed there.

Eleven Bedworth men became casualties in Mesopotamia. Seven men whose graves are not known are recorded on the Basra Memorial, Corporal Lawrence Austin is buried in one of 2,551 burials in Basra Cemetery and Private Arthur Crutchlow, Private Edward A. Ford, Private Charles Sidney Arnold and Private Sam Davenport are four of the 4,621 graves in Amara War Cemetery. One or more of the men could have been originally buried elsewhere as 3,000 graves were brought into the cemetery after the Armistice. All those buried in Basra and Amara cemetery have no headstones as the salts in the soil caused them to deteriorated; they are commemorated on screen walls.

Private Joseph Long, 10992, 9th Bn., Royal Warwickshire Regiment was killed in action, Mesopotamia on the 10th August, 1915, aged 26. Joseph was born in Bilston, Staffordshire to Edward and Sarah Jane Long, who later resided at 9, Mill Street, Bedworth and he enlisted in Nuneaton. Joseph's obituary appeared in '*The Coventry Graphic'*, 19th January, 1917 and '*Nuneaton Observer'*, 5th January, 1917 under the headline '*Bedworth Soldier Killed*' announced: "*Mrs. Long, has received news from the War Office of the death of her son Joseph Long. He joined the 9th Royal Warwick's on 8th of February 1915, was sent to the Dardanelles about June the same year, and was reported missing on August 10th. Nothing more was heard of him until a few days ago, when his death was reported. His mother has received a letter of sympathy from his Majesty the King. Deceased would have been 26 years of age on January 2nd.*"

Joseph is commemorated on the Basra Memorial and his name recorded in 'Fallen Heroes' and on the Bedworth War Memorial.

The Battalion War Diary records; "*Early on the morning the Turks attacked with disastrous results for the Warwickshire Regiment. It was found impossible to hold the line with no supports immediately available. The trenches were enfiladed with machine gun fire and our troops were mown down. Killed 4 Officers, 44 other ranks. Wounded Officers 4, 147 other ranks, Missing Officers 1, other ranks 117.*"

Private Benjamin Martin, 12181, 1st Bn., Oxfordshire and Buckinghamshire Light Infantry was killed in action in the Persian Gulf on the 6th April, 1916. Locally Benjamin's name is recorded in 'Fallen Heroes' and the Bedworth War Memorial and on Panel 26 and 63 of the Basra Memorial. He enlisted in Nuneaton.

On the 12th July, 1916, **Corporal Lawrence Austin** 9537, 9th Bn., Royal Warwickshire Regiment died aged 19. Lawrence was a native of Bedworth and the son of Emily Moore (formerly Austin) and David Austin of 6, Oaks Cottage, Croft Road, Bedworth. Lawrence's name is recorded in 'Fallen Heroes' and on the Bedworth War Memorial and he enlisted in Nuneaton. His death was announced in the '*Bedworth and Foleshill News*' on the 23rd September, 1916 and he is buried in Basra War Cemetery.

Four men were killed in action in January, 1917. The first was **Private Arthur Crutchlow,** 15415, 9th Bn., Royal Warwickshire Regiment on the 16th January, 1917 and he was buried in Amara War Cemetery. Arthur was born in Batley, Yorkshire and enlisted in Bedworth although he was a resident of Nuneaton. His name is recorded on the Bedworth War Memorial. The Battalion War Diary Records: "*One Killed. One wounded. Regimental bombers gained more ground in enemy trench and made new sap head where enemy had filled in their trench.*"

Three men were killed on the 25th January, 1917. Private Arthur Hammersley, Private Edward A. Ford and Private Walter Harry Carter, the latter two being in the 9th Bn., Royal Warwickshire Regiment. The *'Battalion War Diary'* for the Royal Warwickshire shows that they were supporting the Worcesters on the right and the North Staffordshire Regiment on the left at Kala Haji Fahan Nullah. The attack, initially successful was counter attacked by the Turks and the Warwicks were called in to support the Worcesters and Staffords who were being overwhelmed. This action drove the Turks back to their second line, however a second Turkish counter attack in great numbers forced the Warwicks to withdraw. Burial parties were send out on the 27th January and the following day casualties for the 9th Battalion were confirmed as killed or died of wounds, 5 Officers, 46 other ranks. 118 wounded and 18 missing.

Private Arthur Hammersley, 27936, 7th Bn., North Staffordshire Regiment. He was born in Bedworth and must have moved away from the district as he enlisted Coalville, Leicestershire and resided in Ibstock, Leicestershire. Arthurs's name is recorded on the Bedworth War Memorial and on the Basra Memorial. Buried in Amara War Cemetery is **Private Edward A. Ford**, 11497, 9th Bn., Royal Warwickshire Regiment. A native and resident of Bedworth, he enlisted in Nuneaton and his name is recorded in 'Fallen Heroes' and on the Bedworth War Memorial.

Private Walter Harry Carter, 12830, 9th Bn., Royal Warwickshire Regiment was the final casualty from Bedworth on the 25th January, 1917. He was born and resided in Bedworth and enlisted in Nuneaton. *'The Nuneaton Observer'*, 16th February, 1917 under the headline *'Bedworth Soldier Killed'* announced : "*We regret to report that Private Walter Harry Carter, of 19 John Street, Newtown, Bedworth, was killed in action on January 25th. He was 28 years of age and a fine specimen of a athletic Warwickshire*

63

miner. A single man, but engaged to be married on June 16th 1915, he gave himself when his country called for men and joined the 9th Royal Warwick's. Previous to enlisting he was employed at Newdigate Colliery . After three months training at home he was sent out with the Expeditionary Force to the Dardanelles, thence going to Egypt and India, and ultimately to Mesopotamia where he was killed in action. Deceased was a well known local footballer and "Val" as he was popularly called, was very popular among his associates in football circles, he made a fine soldier and was a credit to Royal Warwick's." Walter name is recorded in 'Fallen Heroes', on the Bedworth War Memorial and finally on the Basra Memorial.

Two Bedworth men were killed in February. **Private Charles Sidney Arnold,** 14337, 9th Bn., Royal Warwickshire Regiment was killed on the 11th .February, 1917. He was the son of Charles and Ada Arnold, of 53, Wood Street, Collycroft, Bedworth and was born in Bedworth, enlisting in Nuneaton. His name is recorded in 'Fallen Heroes' and on the Bedworth War Memorial. Aged 18 he was one of the youngest men from Bedworth to loose their lives and he is buried in Amara War Cemetery.

Four days later saw the death of **Lance Corporal William Tallis,** 27064, 8th Bn., Welsh Regiment formerly 4422, Royal Warwickshire Regiment who was killed in action. A native of Bedworth and the son of William Tallis, of 2, Spitalfields, King Street, Bedworth he enlisted locally in Nuneaton. William is commemorated on the Basra Memorial, Bedworth War Memorial and in 'Fallen Heroes'.

The last casualty commemorated on the Basra Memorial is Lance **Corporal George William Ayres,** 22345, 9th Bn., Royal Warwickshire Regiment, who died on 23rd June, 1917, aged 32. George was the son of Mr. and Mrs. George William Ayres, of South View, Yaxley, Peterborough, the husband of Beatrice M. Ayres, of 66, Coventry Road, Bedworth and was born at Holme, Huntingdon. He was one of twenty three men who enlisted in Bedworth and his name is recorded in 'Fallen Heroes' and on the Bedworth War Memorial.

Private Sam Davenport, is the last casualty from Bedworth, he had the service number, 4257 with the 9th Bn., Royal Warwickshire Regiment and died of wounds on the 4th December, 1917. Aged 32, he was born in Collycroft, enlisted in Nuneaton and was married to Ellen L. Davenport, of 3, Shaldon Villas, Fellows Road, Cowes, Isle of Wight and is buried in Amara War Cemetery. Sam's name is recorded in 'Fallen Heroes' and on the Bedworth War Memorial.

The Western Front

1914

The first casualty to die on the Western Front was **Private William H. Rowley**, 97, 1st Bn., Royal Warwickshire Regiment who was killed in action, 13th October, 1914. William was born in Stockingford, where he also resided, and enlisted in Nuneaton. His exact grave in Meteren Military Cemetery (made in 1919 by the French authorities) is not known and it is noted he is buried near the spot IV. C. 609. William's name is recorded both in 'Fallen Heroes' and on the Bedworth War Memorial. Meteren was occupied by German forces early in October 1914 and on the 13th October, their entrenched positions covering the village was captured. The village then remained in Allied hands until the German offensive of April 1918. The *'Battalion War Diary'* shows that at 10.00am the enemy retired just outside Meteren, by 10.00pm the village had been taken with the loss of 42 men and 85 wounded, *'A perfect advance by all companies dash and spirit shown by all'*.

The first man commemorated on the Ypres (Menin Gate) Memorial is **Private Samuel Spencer**, 2052, B Company, 2nd Bn., Royal Warwickshire Regiment who was killed in action, on the 24th October, 1914. The Menin Gate is one of four memorials to the missing in Belgian Flanders which cover the area known as the Ypres Salient, and locally Samuel had been reported missing for several months. Aged 25, he was the son of John Spencer of 250, Marston's Lane, Marston Jabbett, Nuneaton. A native of Hangingheaton, Dewsbury, Yorkshire, he enlisted in Nuneaton, but resided in Bedworth where his name is in 'Fallen Heroes' and on the Bedworth War Memorial.

The *'Battalion War Diary'* indicates the 2nd Bn. were ordered to clear a wood and in passing through the wood came under heavy shell fire.

They were then ordered to take a German-occupied farm house but came under fierce rifle and machine gun fire with numerous casualties.

With no known graves, the next two casualties, Private Peter Johnson, killed in action, 30th October, 1914 and Private John Thomas Stokes, killed in action, 30th November 1914 are also commemorated on the Ypres (Menin Gate) Memorial. **Private Peter Johnson**, 5966, 1st Bn., Royal Welsh Fusiliers was born in Nottingham, enlisted Nuneaton and was a resident of Bedworth.

Private John Thomas Stokes, 6505, 1st Bn., Northamptonshire Regiment died aged 33. John was the son of Henry Stokes and Elizabeth Ann Gilkes, of 2, Hatter's Arms Yard, Leicester Street, Bedworth. A native of Rushden, Northamptonshire, he also enlisted in Northamptonshire at Higham Ferrers. His name is recorded in 'Fallen Heroes' and on the Bedworth War Memorial.

The *'Bedworth and Foleshill News'* on the 12th January, 1915 reported the death of Private Stokes; *"Lord Kitchener intimation and sympathy arrived to his Mother Mrs. Gilkes (son by first marriage) earlier that week. Private Stokes had served seven years with the Northamptonshire Regiment and had been employed seven years on active service. He had also served four years in the reserve, John volunteered at the outbreak of war for another four years in the Second Army reserve and proceeded to the front with his regiment on the 5th August. He was in the fighting line all the time of his death. For several years he was in the employ of Mr. Herbert Goode, Builders of Foleshill. He was a single man and completed his 34th year on December, 5th. The deceased has two brother in laws in service, Chris Hallam with the Leicesters and Heram Gregory also with the Leicesters in training getting ready with Kitchener's Army."*

The last death in 1914, was **Private Charles Albert Ison,** 10885, 1st Bn., Coldstream Guards formerly Royal Warwickshire Regiment who was killed in action on the 22nd December, 1914, aged 22. Charles is commemorated on the Le Touret Memorial, a memorial to the missing which covers the arrival of II Corps in Flanders in 1914 to the eve of the Battle of Loos, September, 1915. Charles was the son of Mrs. Dora Ison of 13, Broad Street, Nuneaton, was born in Bedworth and enlisted in Nuneaton.

1915

As trench warfare continued into 1915, the majority of Bedworth casualties have no known grave, and they are commemorated on the Ypres (Menin Gate) Memorial, Le Touret Memorial, Loos Memorial and the Ploegsteert Memorial. The first casualty of 1915 was **Private Thomas Smalley**, 9835, 2nd Bn., Cameroonians, Scottish Rifles, killed in action on the 10th March, 1915 and commemorated on Le Touret Memorial. Son of John and Kate Smalley of 31, Myra Street, Loughborough, he was born in Hucknall, Nottinghamshire, enlisted in Nottingham and resided in Loughborough so his exact association with Bedworth is unknown. T. Smalley is recorded both in 'Fallen Heroes' and the Bedworth War Memorial.

Also commemorated on Le Touret Memorial is **Private Levi Randle,** 6164, 2nd Bn., Leicestershire Regiment, killed in action, 13th March, 1915. Like so many other Bedworth boys he was born in Bedworth, enlisted in Nuneaton and resided in Bedworth. Private Randle is commemorated locally in 'Fallen Heroes' and on the Bedworth War Memorial.

Private John Cassell and Private Charles Hall were killed in action on the 25th and 26th April, 1915 with the 1st Bn., Royal Warwickshire Regiment and both are commemorated on Panel 8, Ypres (Menin Gate) Memorial. **Private John Cassell,** number 4260, was born in Hinckley, enlisted in Nuneaton and resided at Bedworth. His name is recorded in 'Fallen Heroes' and the Bedworth War Memorial. **Private Charles Hall,**

2393, was born and resided in Bedworth but enlisted in Nottingham. Thomas Chas Hall is recorded in 'Fallen Heroes' and on the Bedworth War Memorial as Charles Hall.

The name recorded John Edmands, is recorded on the Bedworth War Memorial and in the 'Fallen Heroes' as serving with Royal Warwickshire Regiment although further details could not be found either with the Commonwealth War Graves. The *'Nuneaton Observer'*, 21st May, 1915 proves this to be a **Private John Edmunds** of 4, Bulkington Lane, Bedworth whose notification of being killed in action was received that week; "*It was first thought that he died in hospital, but Mr. Wm. Johnson MP wrote to the orderly room of the Royal Warwickshire Regiment and received a reply stating he had been killed in action on the 25th/ 26th April, 1915. John had been in the army for a considerable time and gone to the front at the start of the war*", his battalion was not stated and it was likely to have been the 1st.

On the 25th April, the Battalion were ordered to make an attack at 4.30am but due to insufficient shelling and no support being available, the men had to retire. Casualties were heavy, 17 officers and 500 other ranks killed, wounded or missing. The *'Battalion War Diary'* later explains; "*inadvisable to attack enemy position unless a thorough reconnaissance before hand.*"

Casualties with the 1st Bn., Royal Warwicks were mounting and **Private Sydney Ernest Mills**, 1033, was killed in action on the 2nd May, 1915. On this day C and D Companies were heavily shelled in the early morning, three killed and four wounded. Sydney was the brother of William Thomas Mills, of 56, Mill Street, Bedworth and born in Daventry. He enlisted in Nuneaton and resided in Daventry, although it is possible he spent some time with his brother in Bedworth. He is commemorated on the Ypres (Menin Gate) Memorial.

Back to the Le Touret Memorial with the commemoration of **Private John Padbury Friswell,** 12207, 2nd Bn., Oxfordshire and Buckinghamshire Light Infantry, killed in action on the 16th May, 1915. John was a native of Bedworth, where he also resided, and enlisted in Nuneaton. He is locally recorded in 'Fallen Heroes' and on the Bedworth War Memorial.

The fifth casualty of 1915 with the 1st Bn., Royal Warwickshire Regiment was **Private Thomas Walker,** 4498, on the 3rd June, 1915, aged 27. Thomas was the husband of Edith Ellen Walker of 64, Fitton Street, Nuneaton where he also enlisted. He was born in Sutton Cheney, Market Bosworth, and commemorated in 'Fallen Heroes', on the Bedworth War Memorial and the Ypres (Menin Gate) Memorial.

Eight days later on the 11th June, **Private Abram Ralley,** 1980, 2nd Bn., Royal Warwickshire Regiment was killed in action, aged 33. His father was also called Abram Ralley and his mother, Elizabeth, resided at 2, John Street, New Town, Bedworth where he was also born. He was married to Mrs. H. L. Ralley, of 6, Thomas Street, New Town, Bedworth and enlisted in Nuneaton. Abram's name is recorded in 'Fallen Heroes', on the Bedworth War Memorial and on the Le Touret Memorial.

The third casualty of June 1915 at the Western Front was **Private Isaac Leach,** 19821, 2nd Bn., Wiltshire Regiment formerly 4441, Royal Warwickshire Regiment on the 15th .A resident of Bedworth, he enlisted and resided in Nuneaton. Isaac's name is recorded in 'Fallen Heroes' and on the Bedworth War Memorial locally and also commemorated on the Le Touret Memorial.

Lance Corporal William Henry Stokes and **Rifleman Joseph Sedgwick** are remembered on the Ypres (Menin Gate) Memorial. William, 10469, 3rd Bn., Worcestershire Regiment was killed in action on the 16th June, 1915. He was born locally in Bulkington, enlisted in Warwick and was a resident of Nuneaton. **Lance Corporal William Henry Stokes** name is recorded in 'Fallen Heroes' as W. E. and on the Bedworth War Memorial correctly as W. H.

Rifleman Joseph Sedgwick, R/7141, 7th Bn., King's Royal Rifle Corps, was killed in action, the following month on the 6th July, 1915, aged 20. His father was also Joseph and his mother, Emily resided at 158, Woodland Road, Bedworth. He was also born in Bedworth and enlisted in Nuneaton. Joseph is recorded in 'Fallen Heroes' and on the Bedworth War Memorial.

The following day, **Private Arthur Stanley Gibberd**, 6457, 1st Bn., Canadian Infantry (Western Ontario Regiment) previously Imperial Yeomanry was listed as killed in action, aged 26. Arthur must have emigrated prior to the war as his parents the Reverend John Edward Gibberd and Elizabeth Jane Gibberd resided at Forest View, Charminster Avenue, Bournemouth. Arthur was born on the 21st December, 1884 in Bedworth and enlisted on the 22nd September, 1914. He was the brother of Frederick Eustace Gibberd who also enlisted with the Canadians. Arthur's name is recorded in 'Fallen Heroes' and on the Bedworth War Memorial. Arthur is buried in Phalempin Communal Cemetery, France. Phalempin remained in German hands during almost the whole of the War.

Lance Corporal Joseph Ludgate, 10658, 5th Bn., Oxfordshire and Buckinghamshire Light Infantry was killed in action on the 11th July, 1915. He was the Son of Ben Ludgate, of 21, Henry Street, Coton, Nuneaton and the husband of Florence Powell (formerly Ludgate), of 76, Bottrill Street, Nuneaton. He was actually born in Coventry and enlisted in Nuneaton. With no known grave he is commemorated on the Ypres (Menin Gate) Memorial and locally in 'Fallen Heroes' and on the Bedworth War Memorial.

The patriotic family were featured in 'The Coventry Graphic' his brothers Private H. Ludgate (middle) and Private G. Ludgate (right) were also in the Oxford and Bucks.

The only casualty from Bedworth in August, 1915 was **Sapper, Harry Jee,** 79911, 170th Tunnelling Coy, Royal Engineers formerly 11329 Coldstream Guards who was killed in action on the 20th August, 1915. Harry was born and enlisted in Nuneaton and his name is recorded in 'Fallen Heroes'.

His death was reported in the 'Nuneaton Observer', dated 3rd September, 1915; "That Sapper Jee of Croxhall Street, Bedworth was killed in France after being there several months. A letter describing his death was received by Mr. G. Jee from Captain of the 170th Company: 'I regret that I have to inform you of the death of your son whilst working in the mine gallery by the explosion of a German mine. His death was instantaneous. Whilst serving with my unit he proved himself a very hard working and capable man and  has given every satisfaction. He was held in high esteem and his loss is mourned by all. I extend to you my deepest sympathy and that of all the ranks under my command. He was buried on the afternoon of the 27th August, 1915 the Church of England Chaplain conducting the burial service. His grave will be marked by a substantial wooden cross and registered by the Graves Registration Commission. His personal effects will be forwarded to you by the Adjutant General'. Sapper Gee was a widower with a son of 13, his death has caused keen sorrow at Bedworth for he was well known". Sapper Jee is one of 816 burials in Cambrin Military Cemetery, France: this was one of the front line cemeteries, being about 800 metres from the front line trenches.

Seven Bedworth men were killed or died of wounds on the 25th September, 1915. This was the first day of the Battle of Loos which lasted until the 19th October, 1915 and accounted for over 50,000 casualties. The first two men featured, Private Jack Abraham Tibbitts and Private Oliver Pickard, were with the 6th Bn., Oxfordshire and Buckinghamshire Light Infantry.

Private Jack Abraham Tibbitts, 11632, was 19 years of age. Jack was the son of Daniel Tibbitts and born in Bedworth. He enlisted in Nuneaton at the outbreak of war and was formerly employed at Courtauld's Ltd. Jacks name is recorded in 'Fallen Heroes' and on the Bedworth War Memorial. He was buried in the Royal Irish Rifles Graveyard in France, so called because it was used at first by the Royal Irish Rifles. His grave was brought into this cemetery after the Armistice.

Private Oliver Pickard is the first commemoration on the Ploegstcert Memorial to the missing. His service number was 11606. Oliver was born in Stockingford, enlisted in and resided in Bedworth and his name is recorded in 'Fallen Heroes' and on the Bedworth War Memorial.

Three of the men killed in the first day of fighting were in the 2nd Bn., Royal Warwickshire Regiment, Private Jesse Haywood, Private Frank Alfred Hobbs and Lance Corporal Stanley Albert Hunt all are commemorated on the Loos Memorial to the missing.

Private Jesse Haywood, No. 4415 died aged 28. Jesse was born in Bedworth to Mrs. Eliza Haywood, of 5, Foster's Yard Roadway, Bedworth. He continued living in Bedworth and enlisted in Nuneaton. Locally his name is recorded in 'Fallen Heroes' and on the Bedworth War Memorial.

Private Frank Alfred Hobbs, 2580, C Coy died aged 20. He was born in Nottingham to Clara Eveline (nee Wingfield) and John Hobbs who later resided at 276 Marston Lane, Marston Jabbett, Nuneaton. Enlisting in Coventry, records show he was a resident of Bulkington. Private Hobbs is recorded in 'Fallen Heroes' and on the Bedworth War Memorial.

Also aged 20 was **Lance Corporal Stanley Albert Hunt**, who was partially named after his father, Albert John and his mother was Lilly Maria Hunt, his parents residing at 66, Leicester Road, Bedworth. Stanley was born in Reading, patriotically enlisted in Warwick and resided in Leamington. His name is recorded in 'Fallen Heroes' and on the Bedworth War Memorial.

The final two men killed on the first day at Loos, were with different regiments; Private Robert Henry Rush 19621, D Coy., 1st Bn., Duke of Edinburgh's (Wiltshire Regiment) formerly 11315, Oxfordshire and Buckinghamshire Light Infantry and Private Joseph Henton, 13630, 5th Bn., Oxfordshire and Buckinghamshire Light Infantry. Both are commemorated on the Ypres (Menin Gate) Memorial.

Private Robert Henry Rush, aged 29 was the son of George and Tamah Rush of Grassmoor, Chesterfield. He was born in Hasland, Derby, enlisted in Nuneaton and his name is recorded on the Bedworth War Memorial.

Private Joseph Henton, aged 37, was the son of Joseph Henton, of Chapel Street, Bedworth and the husband of Martha Hannah Henton, of 10, Church Court Church Street, Bedworth. He enlisted in Nuneaton on the 14th September, 1914 and was born in Bedworth, his name is in 'Fallen Heroes' on the Bedworth War Memorial and on Saint Thomas the Apostle Memorial in Longford. The *'Bedworth and Foleshill News'* dated 3rd June, 1916 explains *"He was originally reported as missing now reported as*

dead. He was formerly employed at the Griff Colliery, he was in the Battle of Loos and other engagements".

Three Bedworth men died in October, 1915. The first was **Private Bert Leach,** 11620, 2nd Bn., Oxfordshire and Buckinghamshire Light Infantry who died of wounds on the 20th October, 1915. He was a native of Cannock where he also resided, but had a connection more locally as he enlisted in Nuneaton and his name is recorded on the Bedworth War Memorial. Private Leach is buried in Chocques Military Cemetery, France and it is probable he died after being treated at No.1 Casualty Clearing Station which was posted nearby.

 **Sergeant Walter Cope**, 11335, 7th Bn., Leicestershire Regiment was killed in action, less than a week later on the 26th October, 1915. He also enlisted in Nuneaton, but was born in Wilnecote, Warwickshire and resided in Warwick. Walter's name is recorded in 'Fallen Heroes' and on the Bedworth War Memorial and he has a grave in Bienvillers Military Cemetery, France. The *'Bedworth and Foleshill News',* 29th January, 1916 reported that Sergeant Cope of 133 Nuneaton Road, Collycroft was killed in action. *"He enlisted on 2nd September, 1911 and prior to enlisting was employed at the sinking operation at the Warwickshire Coal Company, new colliery at Keresley. He was 35 years old and leaves a wife and five children. Prior to going to Keresley he worked at Griff Clara and at Newdigate Colliery. Mrs. Cope has been the recipient of many kind letters, the Chaplain said "his death (by accident) should never have happened in such a way, but he was doing his duty and he will have the reward. His comrades stated he was using a catapult to throw grenades into the German trenches and it must of gone off before he was ready."*

The final casualty of 1915 is **Private Joseph Beasley**, 11323, 7th Bn., Leicestershire Regiment who was killed in action on the 29th October, 1915. He was born in Longford and enlisted in Nuneaton. His name is recorded in 'Fallen Heroes', however reference is made to indicate the

Royal Warwickshire Regiment and no match could be found with this detail, his name is also inscribed on the Bedworth War Memorial. Joseph is buried in Albert Communal Cemetery Extension, France. This particular section of the graveyard was used by fighting units and Field Ambulances from August 1915 to November 1916.

1916

The first death in 1916 came on the 8th February, 1916 when **Gunner Frederick William Fathers**, 43424, 12th New Heavy Bty., Royal Garrison Artillery was killed in action. He was aged 24 and the husband of M. J. Harrsion of 130, High Street South, Rushden, Northants and formerly of 104, Regent Street, Bedworth. Frederick was born in Oxford, enlisted in Nuneaton and resided in  Bicester, Oxon. His name is recorded in 'Fallen Heroes' and on the Bedworth War Memorial. The *'Bedworth and Foleshill News'*, dated 26th February, 1916 covered his death; *"Driver Fathers has been killed he leaves a widow and one child. The information conveyed to his wife by Major J. F. Barrington, stated he was killed by a shell that fell on the hut in which he was sitting with four other men. He did not suffer, he was killed at 5.00pm yesterday and buried at 3.00pm this afternoon."* On his death, he was buried in Suzanne Communal Cemetery Extension, France in a village which had been taken over by British troops in the summer of 1915.

 The youngest Bedworth casualty was **Private Samuel Rowland,** 11266, 11th Bn., Royal Warwickshire Regiment who was just 17 when he was killed on the 14th February, 1916. Samuel was the son of Lewis and Harriett Rowland of 191, Tiverton Road, Bournbrook, Birmingham although he was a native of Nuneaton. *'The Midland Counties'* newspaper covered the death of Samuel under the headline *'Bedworth Soldier Killed. Another Local Hero'*. *Private S. Rowland of 34 Sleaths Yard,*

Bedworth has been killed in action. He was a Nuneaton boy who was living at Bedworth at the time he enlisted in the Royal Warwickshire Regiment. The sad news has been conveyed to his friends in the following letter from Second Lieutenant Kenneth W. Harrisery, dated 14th February, 1916: "I regret to have to inform you of the death of your friend, Pte. S. Rowland who was wounded in the trenches on the 13th of this month. He was buried today with full military honours and he will be sadly missed by his companions and he was a good worker and keen soldier, as his officer will testify." A smaller article also appeared in the 'Bedworth and Foleshill News', 26th February, 1916 about the death of a Nuneaton boy who was living in Bedworth when he enlisted. Samuel is buried in Humbercamps Communal Cemetery Extension and it was known this was being used by field ambulances at this time; his name is recorded in 'Fallen Heroes' and on the Bedworth War Memorial.

Five Bedworth men were either killed or died of wounds in March, 1916. **Private William Nicholls,** 18542, 7th Bn., Yorkshire and Lancaster Regiment died of wounds on the 11th March, 1916, aged 19. William was the son of Benjamin and Martha Nicholls, of 92, Marston Lane, Collycroft, Bedworth and born further afield in West Bromwich. A resident of Bedworth, he enlisted in Nuneaton and his name is recorded on the Bedworth War Memorial . Private Nicholls is one of 593 servicemen of the First World War buried or commemorated in Voormezeele Enclosures No.1 and No. 2 Cemetery.

The following day, **Lance Corporal Thomas Mallabone**, 12694, 11th Bn., Royal Warwickshire Regiment was killed in action, aged 32. He seems to be based locally, he was the son of J. T. Mallabone, of Rowley's Green, Foleshill, Coventry, born in Chilvers Coton and resided in Collycroft. Thomas was one of 1,920 men who enlisted in Coventry and he rests in Bienvillers Military Cemetery, France.

Two Bedworth men died on the 20th March, 1916. One of the men who died of wounds, on the 20th March, 1916 was **Private Albert Charles Piper**, 14323, 2nd Bn., Coldstream Guards who died aged 22. Private Piper is associated with Hounslow, his parents Charles and Edith resided at Wellington Road, he was born in Sunbury, Middlesex and resided in Hanworth, Middlesex. A Midland's connection was evident as he enlisted in Coventry and his name is recorded on the Bedworth War Memorial. Albert is buried in Lijssenthoek Military Cemetery, Belgium and it is known that casualty clearing stations were established in this location due to it's proximity to the front.

Private Herbert A. Farndon, 4275, 2nd Bn., Royal Warwickshire Regiment was killed in action on the 20th March, 1916. A local lad, he was the son of Thomas and Alice Farndon and the husband of Mrs. E. Farndon, of 85, York Buildings, Bulkington Road, Bedworth. Herbert was born in Little Beaton, Warwickshire, enlisted in Nuneaton and his name is recorded in 'Fallen Heroes' and on the Bedworth War Memorial. With Grave Reference D. 12. he is buried in Point 110 New Military Cemetery, France which was named after the contour on a map. The local newspaper covered his death noting he was a miner employed in Exhall Colliery, he was apparently killed by a shell, enlisted at the outbreak of war and was married with four children.

Also reported as being killed by a shell and buried in Point 110 New Military is **Private John Bailey**, 12139, 2nd Bn., Royal Warwickshire Regiment who was killed on the 25th March, 1916 by the bursting of a shell near his dug out. John was aged 24 and the son of David and Sarah Ann Bailey, of 27, Wootton Street, Bedworth. He was born in Longford and worked in Longford as he was employed by the Longford Brick and Tile Co.   Enlisting in Nuneaton, he joined the 2nd Battalion, in March, 1915 and whilst serving was attached to a bombing party.

Lieutenant Fairweather writing to his mother stated "*Your son was a fine fellow - the kind we need. He was a good man, greatly respected and his death is a decided loss to the regiment. He gave his life in the most finest possible manner.*" Private Bailey's name is recorded in 'Fallen Heroes' and on the Bedworth War Memorial.

One Bedworth casualty occurred in April, 1916 that of **Guardsman Harry Edward Hartopp**, 17785, 2ⁿᵈ Bn., Grenadier Guards who was killed in action on the 14ᵗʰ April, 1916. As he was born in Bedworth, family or friends arranged for his name to appear on the Bedworth War Memorial and he enlisted in Nuneaton. *'The Bedworth and Foleshill News'*, 29ᵗʰ April, 1916 under the headline *'Bedworth's Man Tragic End'* states "*He was stationed at Caterham before he was called. He was the eldest son of Mr. Harry Hartopp of 112, Coventry Road, Bedworth. Enlisted at the outbreak of war and went to France in 1915, was gassed at Neuve Chappelle. Aged 28 and single. His Corporal S. Hollingbery said; 'He should have been with*  *me on the Lewis Gun but he was inoculated so kept behind when we went to the firing line, he rejoined on the 13ᵗʰ and when I last saw him he said "I Have some letters for you, Sid and there is one from our Lizzie". At 11.30pm one of my men came to tell me he had been shot in the neck and died instantly.* Harry is buried in Menin Road South Military Cemetery, Belgium.

On the 19ᵗʰ May, 1916 a resident and native of Astley, **Private George Treadwell**, 13553, 2ⁿᵈ Bn., Coldstream Guards died in service and was buried at Potijze Burial Ground Cemetery, Belgium and this town is known to have had an Advanced Dressing Station nearby and to have been reachable by enemy shell fire. George enlisted in Nuneaton and his name is recorded in 'Fallen Heroes' and on the Bedworth War Memorial.

Prior to the start of the Battle of the Somme, **Private William Allton**, 15280, 1st Bn., Royal Warwickshire Regiment was killed in action, on the 21st June, 1916. aged 18. He was a son of Thomas and Maria Allton, of 14, Woodlands Road, Bedworth and born on the 2nd May, 1898 at Bedworth. William was employed at Newdigate Colliery as a Packing Case Maker until enlisted in October, 1915 at Nuneaton, seeing active service from April, 1916. William was the brother of Private Joseph Allton who was also killed and along with his brother his name is recorded in 'Fallen Heroes' and on the Bedworth War Memorial. William is buried in Auchonvillers Military Cemetery, France.

The 1st July, 1916 was the start of the Battle of the Somme. Thirteen divisions of Commonwealth forces launched an offensive on a line from north of Gommecourt to Maricourt. Despite a preliminary seven day bombardment, the German defences were barely touched and the attack met unexpectedly fierce resistance. In the following months until the 18th November, 1916 huge resources of manpower and equipment were deployed in the Somme area. (Not all deaths in the Western Front during this period were associated with the Battle of the Somme). At the end of September, Thiepval an original objective of 1st July, was finally captured. Thiepval is synonymous with the Thiepval Memorial which covers over 73,000 men who have no known grave and died in the Somme sector before 20th March 1918 prior to the German offensive.

Two Bedworth men were killed on the first day of the Somme, which saw over 50,000 casualties for the British Army. **Private Joseph Randle**, 12/1298, 12th Bn., King's Own Yorkshire Light Infantry was born in Bedworth and enlisted in Castleford. Joseph was buried in Euston Road Cemetery, Colincamps, France a front line burial ground used during and after the unsuccessful attack on Serre on the 1st July and his is one of the original 501 burials.

 The other casualty on the 1st July was **Private Reuben Kimberley,** 4303, 1/7th Bn., Royal Warwickshire Regiment, aged 29. Reuben was married to Edith of 1, Collingham Row, Newark although he enlisted in Coventry on May the 28th 1915, he resided in Bedworth where his name is in 'Fallen Heroes' and the Bedworth War Memorial. He left not only his widow but also a child. He has no known grave. Reuben is the first Bedworth man commemorated on the Thiepval Memorial, over 90% of those commemorated died between July and November 1916.

The Battalion War Diary records *"Fine Day. This Battalion's role is to hold G sector trenches the left of the 4th Army attack being on our immediate right. We let off smoke and phosphorus bombs to mask fire of enemy opposite us. Our troops met with successes at first – many conflicting reports come through during day. We provided a party of 65 other ranks and 1 Officer to carry up ammunition for 4" stokes guns which were to move forward when flank consolidated, but as no consolidation took place they did not leave our trenches. There were 19 casualties of whom four were killed in this party. In the two coys holding our trenches there were only three casualties all day. No Mans land on our right strewn with bodies after the attack. Many wounded try to crawl back and are sniped at. Many stragglers and wounded during the morning and are dealt with."*

Three weeks later, *'The Bedworth and Foleshill News'* covered his death and his widow was copied on the following message issued to the troops by Lieut. General Sir Weston dated 4th July, 1916:- *It is difficult for me to express my admiration for the splendid courage, determination and discipline displayed by every officer, NCO and men of the battalion that took part in the great attack on the Beaumont Hamel-Serre position on the 1st July. All observers agree in stating that the various waves of men issued from their trenches and moved forward at the appointed time in perfect order undismayed by the heavy artillery fire and deadly machine gun fire. There were no cowards no waverers and not a man fell out. It was a magnificent display of disciplined courage and the best traditions of the British men....Therefore though we did not do all we had hoped to do you have more then pulled your weight and you and are even more glorious comrades who have proceeded us across the great divide have nobly done your duty. We have got to stick it out and go on hammering. Next time we attack, it please God we will not only pull our weight but will pull off a big thing.*

Reuben Kimberley and his Wife, Edith

The following day **Private Thomas William Walker**, 14728, 2nd Bn., Worcestershire Regiment was killed in action, aged 22. Thomas was the husband of Maggie Walker of 113 Nuneaton Road, Collycroft. He was born close by in Foleshill and enlisted in Coventry. He name was later added to an Addenda Panel on the Loos Memorial.

On the 5th July, 1916 **Private Ernest John Bailey,** 20526, 1st Bn., South Staffordshire Regiment was killed in action. A native and resident of Bedworth, he enlisted in Nuneaton, December 1915. His name is inscribed on the Thiepval Memorial, on the Bedworth War Memorial and in 'Fallen Heroes'. The *'Bedworth and Foleshill News'* reported his death on the 29th July, 1916; *Ernest was the eldest son of Mr. E. J. Bailey, Coalpit Fields, Bedworth and was 19 years of age, he was employed at a Bedworth hat factory.*

Between the 9th and the end of July, a further 15 men would die of wounds or be killed in action. On the 9th July, 1916 one of the casualties was **Lance Corporal John Allen Hobbs,** 4629, 11th Bn., Royal Warwickshire Regiment. John was born in Nottingham, enlisted at Nuneaton and is commemorated on the Thiepval Memorial. His name is recorded in 'Fallen Heroes' and on the Bedworth War Memorial The Battalion were in the vicinity of Contalmaison Wood and found three abandoned 77mm guns. The position of the Royal Warwicks was heavily shelled during the afternoon and night, the total casualties according to the Battalion War Diary were "*4 officers wounded, 10 other ranks killed and 66 wounded.*"

Private Alfred Gibbs, 23752, 9th Bn., Leicestershire Regiment was killed in action on the 14th July, 1916, aged 24 and commemorated on the Thiepval Memorial. Alfred, the son of William and Mary Gibbs, of 38, Bermuda Road, Chilvers Coton where he also resided with his wife, Polly. He was born in Bedworth and enlisted in Hinckley.

Three Bedworth men were killed in action on the 15th July, 1916. **Private Herman Crutchlow**, 9609 and **Private John Thomas Hill**, 16356 died with the 2nd Bn., Royal Warwickshire Regiment and both men are commemorated on Pier and Face 9 A 9 B and 10 B, Thiepval Memorial.

Herman, aged 20 was the son of Joseph Daniel Crutchlow, of 50, Wood Street, Collycroft, Bedworth. A native of Dewsbury, Yorkshire he enlisted locally in Nuneaton and was living in Bedworth: his name is recorded in 'Fallen Heroes' and on the Bedworth War Memorial. Less is known about Private John Thomas Hill, he was born in Bedworth, enlisted and resided in Nuneaton.

The *'War Diary'* notes on the 12th July, 1916 the whole division moved forward and the Battalion bivouacked in Mametz Wood. On the morning of the 14th July, the 20th Brigade attacked the German second line trenches and the 22nd Brigade with the 2nd Bn Royal Warwicks leading followed up. After fighting severe fighting around Circus Trench the battalion pushed onto Bazentin-le-Grand village. All four companies had a bad time in the village due to shelling, but dug in and consolidated. This position was held until relieved on the 16th. The casualties were killed 21, wounded 142and missing 62.

The next casualty was a recipient of the Military Medal, **Corporal Cyril Morson Page, MM**, 1622, 1/7th Bn., Royal Warwickshire Regiment who was the final casualty of the 15th July. Aged 19, he was born in Bedworth, the son of Thomas Joseph and Ellen Page, of 134, Edward Street, Nuneaton where he also enlisted. With no known grave he is commemorated on the Thiepval Memorial.

At 12.30am a small party of men were tasked with putting out of action a machine gun which was in a small wood south west of Pozieres but were driven back by the enemy. At 1.30am another party ascertained the enemy were still holding their trenches. In the afternoon at 3.30pm the two platoons were ordered to attack the enemy position on the opposite ridge. The Battalion War Diary records; "*They had scarcely left our trenches when a heavy fire from hostile machine guns was opened on them.*

The fire was so terrific that only the first leading men were able to leave the trench and they were mown down".

Corporal William John Allen, 3660, 2nd /7th Bn., Royal Warwickshire Regiment died of wounds, on the 16th July, 1916 presumably received in the recent fighting. He was aged 32 and the son of William and Sarah Allen, of Bedworth. William married locally to Amy Allen, of Sandpit, Bulkington, he was born in Bedworth and enlisted in Coventry. *'The Bedworth and Foleshill News' dated 29th July, 1916 stated he died from wounds in the advance and formerly worked at the Charity Colliery. "He was very prominent in church life at Bulkington and the 'Dead March' was played at the close of morning service. He had regular correspondence to the vicar and his last letter was read out on the 13th July which read 'Tell the Bulkington people not to fear God". Mr Allen was the originator of the Boy Scouts in Bulkington and they played the last post. He was the brother of Mrs. E. A. Farr, Fruiterer, Newdigate Street, Nuneaton'.* His name is recorded in 'Fallen Heroes' and on the Bedworth War Memorial, he is buried in Laventie Military Cemetery. This cemetery was begun in June 1916, by the 61st (South Midland) Division.

Two more men died on the 16th July, 1916 and are commemorated on the Thiepval Memorial; **Private John Knight**, 11362, 190th Coy., Machine Gun Corps (Infantry) formerly 10990, Royal Warwickshire Regiment and **Private William Harrison**, 14833, 11th Bn., Royal Warwickshire Regiment. John was born and resided in Bedworth, enlisted in Nuneaton and his name is recorded in 'Fallen Heroes' and on the Bedworth War Memorial. William was also born and resided in Bedworth, although he enlisted in Warwick.

The 11th Bn., War Diary shows on the 16th July that they were relieved by the Northumberland Fusiliers after a unsuccessful attack on the previous day on Pozieres. Forty eight percent, 270 out of 580 men were lost by the Royal Warwicks. Pozieres had been reported as thinly held with no wire. In fact the wire in front of the village was not cut and machine guns were in great force.

Six Bedworth men were killed in action on the 19th July, 1916. Five of the men were in the 2/7th Bn., Royal Warwickshire Regiment and commemorated on the Loos Memorial; Private, Alexander Grant Neale, Private Thomas Tallis, Private Tom Whitcroft, Private Aubrey Topp and Private Harold Bates.

The 'Battalion War Diary' states the attack on the 19th commenced at 6.00pm and withdrawal began at 8.10pm. The Battalion had reached Laventie at 7.45am in the morning and were sent up to the front line trenches without loss. A report from Lieutenant Crombie was received at 9.45pm; "Germans have manned their front line trenches and those who went over first are no more". The losses were 13 Officers and 370 other ranks, wounded, killed or missing. During the attack on the 19th July, parties from the Royal Engineers were engaged, they were to be used for consolidation after objectives had been gained. On the 22nd July the diary indicates 50 men were returned to the Mining Company .

In 2009 work began to on an archaeological excavation of a mass grave at Fromelles. The remains of around 400 Australian and British soldiers are believed to be buried in the pits, after the excavation work is completed and the bodies exhumed the men will be given individual burials with military honours at a new cemetery site near Fromelles.

The UK's Veterans Minister Kevan Jones said: "By the end of the project in 2010 all the bodies will be permanently laid to rest in individual graves at a new Commonwealth War Graves Cemetery at Fromelles. Wherever it is possible to identify the remains, named graves will be provided." The names of Private, Alexander Grant Neale, Private Thomas Tallis, Private Tom Whitcroft and Private Harold Bates have been published as possibly being amongst those buried.

Private Alexander Grant Neale, 266506 enlisted in Coventry and was a resident of Bedworth with his name recorded in 'Fallen Heroes' and on the Bedworth War Memorial. **Private Thomas Tallis,** 4233, aged 19 was the son of Zilla and Harry Tallis, of 118, Coventry Road, Bedworth where he also resided. Thomas enlisted in Coventry and is recorded in 'Fallen Heroes' and on the Bedworth War Memorial.

Private Tom Whitcroft, 266485, enlisted in Coventry and resided in Bedworth. Tom's name is recorded in 'Fallen Heroes' and on the Bedworth War Memorial. **Private Aubrey Topp** (machine gunner) was reported locally as dying whilst a prisoner of war on the 1st December 1916. He was born in 1891 and resided and enlisted in Coventry. His father was Joseph Topp who resided at Coundon Road, Coventry (formerly Bedworth).

More information appeared in the local papers about **Private Harold Bates**, 3435. He was aged 27 and the second son of Henry (Jack) Bates (Warwickshire County Cricket grounds man) , of 72, Fitton Street, Nuneaton. Harold was married to Annie Sedgley (formerly Bates), of 127, Corporation Cottages, Holbrook Lane, Coventry  where he enlisted although he was a native of Bedworth. His name is recorded in 'Fallen Heroes' and on the Bedworth War Memorial. Perhaps due to the influence of his father, Harold was one of six Warwickshire County Cricket players who joined the Royal Warwicks in September, 1914. He was a left handed bowler and in the years prior to the war was a member of the Lords Ground staff, with a cricket gene his younger brother Len also played in several Warwickshire matches in 1913 and 1914.

The last casualty on the 19th July, 1916 was **Sapper Frank Pullin**, 132379, 180th Tunn. Coy., Royal Engineers who died aged 31, he is commemorated on the Thiepval Memorial. Frank was the son of John and Eliza Pullin and married to Phyllis Dobney (formerly Pullin). After the war she resided at 85, Analey Road, Stockingford. Frank was born in Tamworth, enlisted in Bedworth and a resident of Nuneaton.

Gunner William Worthington, 1200, "D" Bty. 88th Bde., Royal Field Artillery was killed on the 24th July 1916, aged 20. He was born in Bedworth and resided with his parents , John and Eliza Worthington, of 61, Heath Road, Bedworth. William enlisted in Nuneaton and his name is recorded in 'Fallen Heroes' and on the Bedworth War Memorial. Gunner Worthington is buried in Flatiron Copse Cemetery, this name given by the army to a small plantation a little to the east of Mametz Wood. The ground was taken by the 3rd and 7th Divisions on 14th July 1916 and an advanced dressing station was established.

On the 30th July, 1916, **Private George Bowers**, 14400, was killed in action with the 10th Bn., Royal Warwickshire Regiment. George a native of Denby, Yorkshire, enlisted in Nuneaton and was a resident of Bedworth. With no known grave he is commemorated on the Thiepval Memorial, in 'Fallen Heroes' and on the Bedworth War Memorial.

Thirteen Bedworth men became casualties in August, 1916. The first was **Private Walter Morson**, 29551, 14th Bn., Worcestershire Regiment who died of wounds on the 7th August, 1916, aged 27. Walter was the son of Samuel and Dinah Morson, of 119, Bulkington Road, Bedworth and he was born in Bulkington. His name is recorded both in 'Fallen Heroes' and on the Bedworth War Memorial and he is buried in Longuenesse (St. Omer) Souvenir Cemetery. Throughout the war St. Omer had numerous hospital centres and Casualty Clearing Stations.

Private Charles Joseph Lenton, 1545, 4th Coy., Australian Machine Gun Corps was killed in action on the 9th August, 1916. He emigrated from Bedworth to Australia, and his name is Name recorded in 'Fallen Heroes' and on the Bedworth War Memorial. He is one of 10,770 Australians named on their national memorial to the missing at Villiers-Bretonneux. Joseph enlisted on the 3rd November, 1914 in Australia and was previously employed as confectioner in Nuneaton. During the Gallipoli campaign he was registered as sick and sent to hospital on the 5th July, 1915 until the 5th February, 1916 when he rejoined his unit. On the 1st June, 1916 he was send to France and disembarked on the 9th June, 1916 at Marseilles. On his death, his possessions (ID disc and

Prayer book) were sent to his mother, Norah Lenton at 57, King Street, Bedworth. By the 14th September, 1916 the Australian Archives state *"Killed in action. No trace can be found."*

Four days later on the 13th August, 1916 three Bedworth men were killed with the 11th Bn., Royal Warwickshire Regiment, all are commemorated on the Thiepval Memorial and locally in 'Fallen Heroes' and on the Bedworth War Memorial. All three men enlisted in Nuneaton. **Private, William Smith**, 12661, was the eldest of the three men at 43. A native of Bedworth, William was married to Emma Smith, of 4, Mill Cottages, Hill Street, Collycroft, Bedworth. **Private Richard Thorpe**, 17378, was born and resided in Bedworth. The final casualty with the 11th Bn., was **Lance Corporal Albert Arthur Gammage**, 17916, who was aged 23. Albert (Known as Bert) was born in Abbington, Northamptonshire to Alfred George and Mary Jane Gammage; they later resided at 14, Wood Street, Rugby. Bert was married to Ellen Beatrice Gammage of 186, Tomkinson Road, Stockingford, Nuneaton.

The *'War Diary'* on the 12th August states that zero hour occurred at 10.30pm. The preceding bombardment advertised the attack and 77mm shrapnel fire and machine gun fire was opened up on the men. Other ranks killed 11, wounded 100 and missing 37. The diary for the following day shows that men were returning to the trenches and the wounded recovered; *"The Germans showed themselves, shouted friendly remarks and appeared anxious for anxious for a peaceful spell."*

On the 18th August, 1916, **Private Harry Everitt**, 201736, (6009), 1st/5th Bn., Royal Warwickshire Regiment was killed in action, aged 34. A native of Bedworth, he enlisted in Warwick and his parents were Thomas and Ada Everitt, of 36, Newtown Road, Bedworth. With no known grave his name is inscribed on the Thiepval Memorial and the Bedworth War Memorial, and recorded in 'Fallen Heroes'.

The Battalion were stationed at Orvillers Post and a successful attack recorded. A Coy took the first objective and B Coy took the second. The success in the War Diary is associated with ladders being placed at the 'jumping off' point during the previous night.

Three Bedworth men died with the 5th Bn., Oxfordshire and Buckinghamshire Light Infantry on the 24th August 1916.

Commemorated on the Thiepval Memorial and recorded in 'Fallen Heroes' and on the Bedworth War Memorial is **Private Thomas Tidman,** 11390. Thomas was named after his father, and his mother was Mary Ann Tidman. His parents resided at 13A, Roadway, Bedworth. Thomas was born in Bedworth and was killed in action, aged 22. Thomas was an employee of the Exhall Colliery prior to enlisting in Nuneaton.

Private Edgar Percival Cater, 21790, has a known grave in Delville Wood Cemetery. Delville Wood was an area of woodland, which touched the village of Longueval in the Somme area. This cemetery was made after the Armistice, when graves were brought in from surrounding cemeteries. Private Cater was killed in action, aged 20. He was the son of J. Cater, of Bedworth and he married locally to Elsie May Cater, of 10, Hayes Lane, Exhall, Coventry. Edgar was born in Wyken, Coventry, resided in Collycroft and enlisted in Nuneaton. His name is recorded in 'Fallen Heroes' and on the Bedworth War Memorial.

The remaining casualty was **Private Joseph Moore,** 19334, aged 40. Joseph has no known grave and is commemorated on the Thiepval Memorial, he enlisted in Nuneaton. Joseph was married to Harriett Moore, of 28, Croft Road, Bedworth Heath, Nuneaton and was a native of Bedworth, as such his name is recorded in 'Fallen Heroes' and on the Bedworth War Memorial.

 Two Bedworth men were killed on the 27th August, 1916 although with different regiments. **Gunner Alfred George Middleton**, 546, "D" Bty. 240th (South Midland) Bde., Royal Field Artillery was killed near Aveluy, France at the age of 23. Alfred was the third son of Edward and Rebecca Middleton, of 78, Richmond Street, Stoke, Coventry formerly of 572, Great Heath, Coventry. He was born in 1893 at Collycroft and resided at 572 Foleshill Road, Coventry as he was employed in the City as an Engineer at the Triumph Works Ltd. He enlisted in October, 1914 and had been in France about 18 months before his death. Alfred was educated at Bablake School, *'where he gave great promise of a very bright future'*. His brother Robert Middleton was a Corporal in the same battery. Major Fowler writing to his parents mentioned *"the deceased was one of the best gunners in the Battery and a popular favourite with officers and men."* The Chaplain (Reverend Cyril. A. Brown writes *"There is not a man in the battery who does not feel his loss"*. Gunner Middleton is one of 613 burials in Aveluy Communal Cemetery Extension, France and is commemorated on the Bablake School Memorial.

The second man is **Private Ernest Musson**, 307648, 1/6th Bn., Royal Warwickshire Regiment who enlisted in Nuneaton and resided at Stockingford. Although his name is recorded local to Bedworth in 'Fallen Heroes' and on the War Memorial, the name of E. Musson appeared on a Roll of Honour in Cathedral Church of St. Michael (unfortunately destroyed during the bombing of Coventry in World War II). Ernest has no known grave and is commemorated on the Thievpal Memorial. On the 27th the battalion were resting at Bouzincourt, with one casualty and six wounded the previous day whilst in the trenches.

 Also on the Thiepval Memorial is **Private Arthur Smith**, 17832, 15th Bn., Royal Warwickshire Regiment, who died from wounds on the 29th August, 1916, aged 32. Arthur was born in Witherley, Leicestershire to Mrs Eliza Smith of 7, Coventry Road, Bulkington. He enlisted in Nuneaton and resided at Bedworth. *'The Bedworth and Foleshill News'* dated September 9th 1916 reported his death: *"he formerly resided at the Navigation Inn, he had not been at the front very long and had previously been employed in a milk round in Bedworth."* His name is recorded in 'Fallen Heroes' and on the Bedworth War Memorial.

'The Bedworth and Foleshill News' was also responsible for providing details on **Private George T. Randle** dated September 23rd, 1916. This explained *"The deceased, resided with Mrs. Davis and his brother Richard Randle received a letter stating he died of wounds. A rumour spread that he was in York minus a leg but this was unfounded. Private Frank Moreton of Coton Heath End sent a letter home although slight disagreement about the date, saying he had been hit but he did not know how he ended up as he had to go up the line with a fatigue party. Some of the chaps said he was killed but he did send a message down to me saying send my money home. He died soon after receiving his wounds."* Private Randle, 18136, 16th Bn., Royal Warwickshire Regiment actually died of his wounds on the 31st August, 1916. He was the son of Solomon Randle of Nuneaton, a sportsman, he was Captain of the Nuneaton Rugby Football Club. He was born in Nuneaton. George's name is recorded in 'Fallen Heroes', and he enlisted with the Royal Warwicks in Warwick. After succumbing to his wounds he was buried in Peronne Road Cemetery, Maricourt, France which at this time was very near the front line.

With the Battle of the Somme continuing, September 1916 saw the loss of more Bedworth men. The first was **Lance Corporal Thomas Marston**, 14336, 10th Bn., Royal Warwickshire Regiment killed in action on the 1st September, 1916. His death was reported as being due to the bursting of a German grenade and he lived for two minutes after being struck. Thomas was the son of Mr. and Mrs. Marston of Villa Park Road, Bedworth. He enlisted in September, 1915 (aged 17) at Nuneaton and had been in France about five months when he was killed at just 18. He was a native of Bedworth, an employee of Courtaulds and his name is recorded in 'Fallen Heroes'. On his death he was buried in Dranoutre Military Cemetery, Belgium.

Memorial Plaque and medals of Lance Corporal Marston

Eight Bedworth men were listed as killed in action on the 3rd September, 1916 and the majority of these were with the 2nd Bn and 14th Bn. of the Royal Warwickshire Regiment. The 2nd Bn. *'War Diary'* indicates the men had assembled west of Waterlot Farm with zero hour at noon. The objective at the west end of Ginchy was reached, however reports came through that the men were leaving the village and with heavy casualties it was decided to relieve the Brigade. Losses were other ranks, 26 killed, 7 died of wounds, 197 wounded and 90 missing.

Private Alfred Martin, 16379, 2nd Bn., Royal Warwickshire Regiment was aged 21 and the son of Alfred and Ada Martin, of 60, Mill Street, Bedworth. He was born on 18th December, 1893 at Bedworth and enlisted on 30th January, 1916 also at Bedworth. Alfred's name is recorded in 'Fallen Heroes' and he was employed as a Spinner. *'The Bedworth and Foleshill News'* covered his death in December 1916, it reported he had received training at the Isle of Wight and had originally been reported as missing as of 17th September then as killed since 3rd September. He is buried in Serre Road Cemetery No.2, the graves here were brought in from the battlefields of the Somme and Ancre when they were cleared after the Armistice.

Private John Barlow and **Private George Samuel Wilkins** were also with the 2nd Bn., they have no known grave and are commemorated on the Thiepval Memorial. John, service no. 11987, was born in West Bromwich, enlisted in Bedworth and his name is recorded in 'Fallen Heroes' and on the Bedworth War Memorial. The connection of Private Wilkins, 17677, with Bedworth is not so obvious. He was aged 42, the son of William and Mary Wilkins of Occupation Lane, Woodville, Burton-on-Trent and was born in Branston, Staffordshire. He enlisted in Bedworth but records indicate he resided at Woodville, Derbyshire.

Three men also died with the 14th Bn., and 16th Bn., Royal Warwickshire Regiment and all are commemorated on the Thiepval Memorial. **Private Thomas Pegg,** 17497, 14th Bn., was age 36 when he was killed. Thomas was the son of Henry and Eliza Pegg and born in Bedworth although he enlisted in Nuneaton. **Private George Thos. Kemp,** 15281, was also born in Bedworth and enlisted in Nuneaton. A resident of Bedworth, his name is recorded in 'Fallen Heroes' and on the Bedworth War Memorial. The final Royal Warwicks soldier to be killed in action on the

3rd September was **Private Frank Biddle,** service no. 18122, 16th Battalion. Frank was born in Birmingham, enlisted in Warwick and resided in Bedworth where he is commemorated in 'Fallen Heroes' and on the Bedworth War Memorial.

The 16th Battalion War Diary states they were located in Casement Trench and B Company were involved in the attack at 6.30pm, at 6.31pm 'intense enemy machine gun fire' was noted and at 6.55pm a message received saying the attack had failed. At 7.05pm the remaining men were ordered to withdraw.

The final two men killed on the 3rd September were with the Sherwood Foresters and Oxfordshire and Buckinghamshire Light Infantry, both are named on the Thiepval Memorial. The eldest at 39 was **Private William Moore,** 25864, 17th Bn., Sherwood Foresters. William was married to Hannah Moore of 25, Brickyard Road, Butler's Hill, Hucknall. He was born in Bedworth and enlisted in his wife's home town. He was the son of Benjamin and Harriet Moore, prior to the outbreak of war he was employed as a miner. Aged 21, was **Private Charles Henry Goode**, 11612, 6th Bn., Oxfordshire and Buckinghamshire Light Infantry. He lived and was born in Bedworth and like so many other men enlisted in Nuneaton, his father Alfred W. Goode resided at 5, Cleaver's Yard, High Street, Bedworth. Living locally his name is recorded in 'Fallen Heroes' and on the Bedworth War Memorial.

Also with the 6th Bn., Oxfordshire and Buckinghamshire Light Infantry but dying of wounds on the 4th September, 1916 was **Private Arthur Griffiths**, No. 12173. The wounds were probably received on the previous day, he was aged 22. Like Private Goode he was born and lived in Bedworth and enlisted in Nuneaton. His parents were known to reside at Ferndale Cottage, 58, Coventry Road, Bedworth and they were John and Rose Ann Griffiths. His name is recorded on the

Bedworth War Memorial and he has a known grave in Heilly Station Cemetery, Mericourt-L'Abbe, Somme, France. As Arthur died of wounds he was probably treated at either the 36th or 38th Casualty Clearing Station or the 2/2nd London Hospital due to it's proximity at the front: burials were carried out under extreme pressure.

'The Bedworth and Foleshill News' covered his death on the 21st October, 1916; *"The deceased lived at 10 Congrave Square, Bedworth. Enlisted over a year ago in the Worcesters and had been in France ten months. Worked for painter and decorator, Mr. L. J. Bunney, Kenilworth. Letters to parents from Chaplain L. M. Evans, stated "He was in the trenches when a shell burst near his dugout , he suffered no pain. He was buried next day in a little cemetery behind the trenches a wooden cross will be erected....your son died nobly for king and country"*.

Acting Bombardier George Henry Dean, MM. also died on the 4th September, 1916 His service number was 35616, D Bty., 107th Bde., Royal Field Artillery and with no known grave he is commemorated on the Thiepval Memorial. During service he was awarded the Military Medal. Locally his name is recorded in 'Fallen Heroes' and on the Bedworth War Memorial, although he originated from Stafford and enlisted in Doncaster.

Dying of wounds on the 9th September, 1916, aged 20 was **Private John William Spacey,** 11366, 6th Bn., Oxfordshire and Buckinghamshire Light Infantry. He may have also been fatally wounded in the action on the 5th as he died in the district of Rouen and is buried at St. Sever Cemetery,. John was the son of William and Mary Ann Spacey, of 96, Bulkington Lane, Bedworth. A native of Whitwick, Leicestershire, he enlisted in Nuneaton and was a resident of Bedworth. His name is recorded in 'Fallen Heroes' and on the Bedworth War Memorial.

Two Bedworth men were killed in action with the Grenadier Guards on the 14th and 15th September, 1916. The first was with the 3rd Bn., **Guardsman Harry Richards,** 20822, 3rd Battalion who was aged 32.

Harry was married to Esther Richards, of 140, Bulkington Road, Bedworth and his parents, Samuel and Sarah Richards, were also natives of Bedworth. Harry enlisted at Nuneaton and his name is recorded in 'Fallen Heroes' and on the Bedworth War Memorial. Harry is buried in Guards' Cemetery, Lesboeufs, Somme, France. Lesboeufs was attacked by the Guards Division on the 15th September 1916 and captured by them on the 25th and this is how the cemetery took it's name.

Guardsman John Arnold Spencer, 17791, 2nd Bn., Grenadier Guards was killed the following day. John was named after his father who resided at 250, Marston's Lane, Marston Jabbett, Nuneaton. A native of Dewsbury, Yorkshire, he enlisted locally in Nuneaton. Known in Bedworth, his name is recorded in 'Fallen Heroes' and on the Bedworth War Memorial. Although he is buried in a cemetery, he has a special memorial in Serre Road Cemetery, No. 2: the exact location of his grave is in the region of Plot XL. F. 11.

On the 26th September 1916, **Private William Alfred Moore**, 17915, 16th Bn, Royal Warwickshire Regiment died of wounds. He was one of the few men who was born, enlisted and resided in Bedworth. His name is rightfully recorded in 'Fallen Heroes' and on the Bedworth War Memorial. Notification of his death appeared in *'The Bedworth and Foleshill News'* casualty list on the 11th November, 1916 and he is buried in Corbie Communal Cemetery Extension, France. Corbie was basically a medical centre, with the cemetery extension taking men who died of wounds in the Battle of the Somme.

The following day **Rifleman Arthur Edward Hewitt**, R/20351, 3 platoon, A coy., 2nd Bn., King's Royal Rifle Corps was killed in action and is commemorated on the Thiepval Memorial. Arthur was born in Hawkesbury, enlisted on the 30th March, 1916 at Coventry where he worked in the Coventry Co-Operative Bakery Department. He lived at 28

Bulkington Road, Bedworth and his name is recorded in 'Fallen Heroes' and on the Bedworth War Memorial. The family received a letter from Private Leonard Hewitt, which stated; *"We were in the trenches and under constant shell fire, it was from one of the many pieces from these shells that your son was struck and he died instantly."*

Five Bedworth men were either killed or succumbed to wounds in October, 1916. **Acting Corporal William Jacques**, 17667, 9th Bn., West Yorkshire Regiment died of wounds on the 4th October, 1916, aged 38. William was the son of John and Hannah Maria Jacques, of 39, Dolphin Street, Attercliffe, Sheffield although he was born in Bedworth. The family must have moved to Sheffield after William was born and he enlisted and resided in Attercliffe, Sheffield. His name is recorded in 'Fallen Heroes' and on his death he became one of 264 burials in Etretat Churchyard, France. This cemetery was used from December 1914, by the No.1 General Hospital.

Private Arthur Griffin, 22777, 3rd Bn., Worcestershire Regiment was killed on the 9th October, 1916, aged 20. Arthur was the son of Mrs. Maria Griffin, of 58, Marston Lane, Bedworth and was born in Bedworth. He enlisted in Nuneaton and has no known grave so he is commemorated on the Thiepval Memorial. Locally his name is recorded in 'Fallen Heroes' and on the Bedworth War Memorial. Arthur was wounded in the first few days of the Somme and once recovered would have rejoined his regiment.

At the foot of the Thiepval Memorial lies Thiepval Anglo-French Cemetery, buried here is **Private Roland Wilson**, 17967, 1st Bn., Royal Warwickshire Regiment. He was killed in action on the 12th October, 1916, aged 25. He was reported missing in *'The Coventry Graphic'* on the 24th November, 1916 and it was noted that he was employed by Mr. George Rice, painter and decorator prior to enlisting. In the winter of 1931-32, it was decided that a small mixed cemetery be made to represent

98

the loss of both the French and Commonwealth nations. Of the 300 Commonwealth burials in the cemetery, 239 are unidentified. The bodies were found in December 1931 and January-March 1932, the majority coming from the Somme battlefields of July-November 1916. Roland was born in Bulkington, the son of James Wilson of Leicester Street, Bulkington and he also resided at Bulkington with his wife, Annie J. Wilson at 2 Rugby Road, Bulkington although he enlisted in Bedworth.

The Battalion were in trenches east of Les Boeufs and on the night of the 11th/12th October the companies were spread amongst German Trench, Foggy Trench, 25 Trench, Fluffy Trench and Muggy Trench. The artillery started at 7.30am and finished at 2.30pm. With zero hour at 2.05pm the Battalion doubled out of the trenches in four waves and gained No Man's Land. Those attacking on the left were held up by a strong point consisting of heavy machine gun fire and combined with a creeping barrage which got too far ahead the objective could not be obtained. In the attack 5 officers were killed and 259 other ranks casualties.

Gunner Thomas George Hardiman, 10546, C Bty., 58 Bde., Royal Field Artillery had been reported missing since the 21st October, 1916 and it was later reported on the 1st December, 1916 that he had died on this date. Thomas was born in Bedworth and enlisted in Coventry. As a native of Bedworth his name is recorded in 'Fallen Heroes' and on the Bedworth War Memorial and he is buried in Serre Road Cemetery No.2, France.

Buried in Berks Cemetery Extension is **Private Charles Paul Montgomery**, 9396, 2nd Bn., Royal Warwickshire Regiment who was killed in action on the 24th October, 1916. This cemetery was begun in April 1915 by the 1st /4th Royal Berkshire Regiment and the extension was begun in June 1916 and used continuously until September 1917. Private Montgomery was one of the original burials as more graves were added after the Armistice. Charles was born on the 11th November, 1883 in Far Gosford Street Coventry. He also resided in Coventry with

Doncaster stated as his place of enlistment. His association with Bedworth is not entirely clear, although he was employed as a miner and his name is recorded in 'Fallen Heroes' and on the Bedworth War Memorial.

The Thiepval Memorial records the name of **Private Rowland William Hill,** 8693, 10th Bn., Royal Warwickshire Regiment formerly 21355, Hussars. who was killed in action, on the 18th November, 1916. This was the last official day of the Battle of the Somme. Rowland was born in Yardley, Birmingham, enlisted in Nuneaton and was a resident of Bedworth. He is commemorated in 'Fallen Heroes' and on the Bedworth War Memorial.

Private William George Hastings, 10087, 11th Bn., Royal Warwickshire Regiment died of wounds, on the 22nd November, 1916, aged 24. His wounds were probably received during the Battle of the Somme. William was born in Coleshill to George and Mary Ann Hastings, who later resided at 35, Smorrell Lane, Bedworth. He enlisted in Coventry and his name is recorded in 'Fallen Heroes' and on the Bedworth War Memorial. He is buried in Boulogne Eastern Cemetery. During the war, Boulogne, was one of the three base ports, the majority of those who died in hospitals at Boulogne were buried in this cemetery.

The last casualty recorded on the Thiepval Memorial for 1916 is **Private, Thomas Moore**, 6462, 1/5th Bn., Royal Warwickshire Regiment who was killed in action on the 8th December, 1916. He enlisted in Bedworth and records show he resided at Longford, Coventry and has his name inscribed on Saint Thomas the Apostle Memorial in Longford. The Battalion 'War Diary' indicates the Battalion were located at Le Sars & Acid Drop Camp Martinpuich. On the 8th they were relived by the 1/8th Royal Warwicks in the front line trenches and moved back to shelters and dug-outs in Martinpuich. Casualties 1other rank killed and 1 other rank wounded.

The last casualty of 1916 was **Private Frederick Picker,** 11384, 3rd Bn., Coldstream Guards who died of wounds on the 12th December, 1916.

Aged 21. A resident of Bedworth, he enlisted at Nuneaton and was the son of John and Elizabeth Picker. The family must have moved to the area as he was born in Mansfield. Frederick is recorded in 'Fallen Heroes' and on the Bedworth War Memorial and is buried in Grove Town Cemetery, France. This was used to deal with casualties from the Somme battlefields by the 2/2nd London Casualty Clearing Stations.

1917

The first two casualties of 1917 were buried in Vieille-Chapelle New Military Cemetery, France which was used by fighting units and Field Ambulances, their graves are original burials - graves were added after the Armistice. **Lance Corporal William Joseph Priest, MM** who died on the 29th January, 1917 aged 45. His service no was 11038 with the 11th Bn., Royal Warwickshire Regiment. William was the son of Thomas and Harriet Priest, of Bedworth, born in Bedworth and his work took him to Hucknall, Nottinghamshire where he enlisted. *'The Nuneaton Observer'* on the 2nd March, 1917 under the headline *'Bedworth Soldier's Death'* records: *"News has reached Bedworth of the death which took place on January 29th of an old Bedworth soldier, Corporal William John Priest. Deceased was born at Bedworth and lived there up to a few years ago, when he left the Newdigate Colliery and went to work in Notts Coalfield. He enlisted in the 11th Royal Warwicks at the outbreak of war and had been at the front for a year and eight months. He was at Beaumont Hamel at the time of his death, being seized with illness in the trenches. In less then half an hour he died. He had been decorated in the field for bravery with the Military Medal."* His death was covered in the March edition of the *'Bedworth and Foleshill* News' with the additional information that he had worked at Courtaulds.

His name is duly recorded in 'Fallen Heroes' and on the Bedworth War Memorial, it is also known that his brother attended a ceremony for wounded or deceased soldiers at Bournbrook 1st Southern General Hospital given by Major General Western MM.

Three days later came the death of **Private Ernest Payne,** 65219, 112th Coy., Machine Gun Corps (Infantry) formerly 35324, Worcestershire Regiment. He died aged 24. Ernest was the son of Thomas and Sarah S. Payne, of 4, Long Street, Ryton, born in Bulkington and was one of the twenty three casualties who enlisted at Bedworth.

Killed in action, in the vicinity of Grandcourt on the 5th February, 1917 was **Private John Thomas Spencer,** 35911, 14th Bn., Worcestershire Regiment, aged 19. John was born on 6th November, 1897 at Bedworth to John Henry and Elizabeth Spencer, of 67, Park Road, Bedworth. He enlisted in Coventry in August, 1916 and was employed at Coventry Ordnance Works formerly Courtaulds. He continued residing in  Bedworth and his name is recorded in 'Fallen Heroes' and on the Bedworth War Memorial. With no known grave he is commemorated on the Thiepval Memorial. The *'Bedworth and Foleshill News'* covered his death in March 1917.

 The only Officer from Bedworth who became a casualty was **Second Lieutenant Tom Freeman,** 6th Bn., Northamptonshire Regiment attached 54th Trench Mortar Battery. Tom was killed in action near Miraumont on the 17th February, 1917, aged 22. He was named after his father, and his mother was Mary Freeman (Mockford), his parents resided at Wootton Street, Bedworth. Tom was married Hilda Frances Freeman (Skipper), of 132, King Edward Road, South Hackney, London. While a scholar at a Bedworth Elementary School he won a county scholarship and went to Nuneaton Grammar School where he was in the cricket and football teams. A further scholarship took him to

University College (London) and he secured a commission soon after the outbreak of war.

A letter received by his widow from his Captain states *"Your husband has earned a splendid reputation amongst us for his fearlessness in the most trying circumstances, and in him we have lost an officer who had won the confidence and affection of all who knew him."* 'The Coventry Graphic' commented in March, 1917: *"Everyone who knew Lieutenant Freeman feels that a most promising and brilliant career has been cut short by his untimely death."* Second Lieutenant Freeman's name is recorded in 'Fallen Heroes' and on the Bedworth War Memorial and he is buried in Regina Trench Cemetery, Grandcourt, Somme, France. The cemetery was completed after the Armistice when graves were brought in from the battlefields of Courcelette, Grandcourt and Miraumont. He is not buried in one of the original plots it is probable his grave came in after the Armistice.

With no casualties in March, 1917 the next two casualties came on the 10th April, 1917 with the 11th Bn., Royal Warwickshire Regiment. **Private Joseph Rider,** 28555, was killed in action, aged 19. His parents resided at 246, Marston Lane, Bedworth and he was named after his father, his mother was Lucy Charlotte Rider. Joseph was born in Coventry, enlisted in Warwick and resided in Bedworth. He is commemorated in 'Fallen Heroes' and on the Bedworth War Memorial. **Corporal Thomas Bramley,** 12637, was killed aged 18. Thomas was the son of Mrs. Elizabeth P. Bramley and born in Jekinston, Derbyshire. A resident of Bedworth, he enlisted in Nuneaton and his name is recorded in 'Fallen Heroes'.

Both Private Rider and Corporal Bramley are commemorated on the Arras Memorial, which records almost 35,000 servicemen who died in the Arras sector between the spring of 1916 and the 7th August 1918 (the eve of the Advance to Victory) and have no known grave. The most conspicuous events of this period were the Arras offensive of April-May 1917.

On the 11th April 1917, two Bedworth men were killed with 1st Bn., Royal Warwickshire Regiment. **Private Harry Butler**, 13071, was born and resided in Bedworth and enlisted in Nuneaton. Private Butler's name is recorded in 'Fallen Heroes' and on the Bedworth War Memorial. On his death he was buried in Athies Communal Cemetery Extension, France. Athies was captured on the 9th April, 1917 , on it's capture the extension of the communal cemetery was begun and used by field ambulances and fighting units, Private Butler is one of 312 burials. **Private Frederick Sparrow**, 16190 was born at Chilvers Coton and enlisted in Bedworth. His name is recorded in 'Fallen Heroes' and on the Bedworth War Memorial.

Private Sparrow is buried in Grave Ref. II. D. 26. at Browns Copse Cemetery, Roeux, France. Plot II indicates this was one of the graves cleared from the battlefield in the summer of 1917. Roeux was built over a system of caves which helped to make its capture from the Germans in April 1917 exceptionally difficult, attacks on the 12th April failed and it was not taken until the 22nd April, 1917.

At noon on the 11th an attack by the Royal Irish Fusiliers and 2nd Seaforth Highlanders had started from the east edge of Fampoux, the 1st Battalion were following but were heavily shelled in the assembly position prior to the attack and had many casualties. The attack was then held up by machine gun fire. The *'Battalion War Diary'* records *'it was very cold and snow'*.

 The next casualty was also with the 1st Bn., Royal Warwickshire Regiment, **Private Amos Twigger**, 4423, B Coy. who was killed in action on the 17th April, 1917. Amos was named after his father and his mother was Jane Twigger, his parents resided at 17, Bath Road, Nuneaton. Private Twigger's name is recorded in 'Fallen Heroes' and on the Bedworth War Memorial. With no known grave he is commemorated on the Arras Memorial.

'The Nuneaton Observer', headline 'Nuneaton Soldier Killed. A former Bedworth Resident'; "Mr. Twigger of 296, Gadsby Street, Nuneaton has just received news that his son, Private Amos Twigger (late of Bedworth) was killed in action, in France on April 17th. He enlisted in the 1st Royal Warwicks immediately war was declared, and has seen a good deal of hard fighting. He was only 22 years of age. He was a miner and worked for the Griff Colliery Ltd at their 'Clara' Pit. We understand that considerably over 100 men from the Griff Colliery Company have given their lives for the country. Private Twigger is one of a family of ten children, and has a brother also on active service in Salonika. He was associated with the Bedworth Wesleyan Sunday School for many years. The following letter has been received by friends of the deceased – My Dear Friends – As regards to news of your son, Amos. Well all that I can tell you is that he was killed instantly by a German shell on the 17th April, 1917.

During the bombardment and just before he got hit one of our fellows said to him "Come along the trench a little, Amos," so he said "Oh, I shall be alright here," and the next we heard was that he was killed, so I take these to be his last words and concerning his photos and cigarette case I saw the fellows today that buried him and they told me that they were unable to take anything from him owing to the intense shelling, so you can gather from this that all his belongings were buried with him. Well, friends I am sure you have my deepest sympathy and the fellows in his section send the same, as he was very well admired by all who knew him, both Officers, NCO's and men. So now I think this is as much as I can possibly tell you and I hope I hear again from you in the near future also Dinah. Give my best love to Norman and the rest of your children and accept same yourself. From your sincere Friend. Corporal Leach, B Coy., 1st Royal Warwicks, B. E. F, France.

A letter of condolence from Sergeant F. Adams added "He was well liked by everyone in the Company and always performed his duties required of him in a cheerful and efficient manner. I have known him the whole of the time he was in France and during that period he was one of the Lewis gun team under me. He was an excellent man with the gun and always did utmost to give satisfaction. We buried him as soon as we could after his death." A letter from Second Lieutenant H. J. Dixon expresses heartfelt sympathy as he was his Platoon Commander for more then six months, but points out *"he was temporarily detached to another company and only heard of his death when we came out."*

The medals of Private Amos Twigger

There were three more casualties before the end of April and they are all commemorated on the Arras Memorial. **Private Benjamin Edwards,** 17822, 10th Bn., York and Lancaster Regiment was killed in action on the 21st April, 1917. Benjamin was born in Bedworth although he enlisted further afield in Attercliffe, Sheffield. His name is recorded on the Bedworth War Memorial.

A week later saw the death of **Private Herbert Harry Carter**, G/51913, 17th Bn., Royal Fusiliers who was killed in action near Oppy Wood on the 28th April, aged 28. Herbert was the son of Henry and Mary Ann Carter, of Rectory Cottage, Exhall, Coventry and born on 22nd September, 1888 at Great Malvern. He enlisted in Bedworth in January, 1916. Private Carter's name is recorded in 'Fallen Heroes' and on the Bedworth War Memorial.

Also on the 28th was the death of **Private Charles Frederick Horner,** 44163, 24th Bn., Northumberland Fusiliers formerly 80887, East Yorkshire Regiment. Charles was born in Ikley, Yorkshire and enlisted in Coventry, he may have resided in Bedworth as his name is recorded on the Bedworth War Memorial.

From action on the 3rd May, 1917 two more Bedworth names would later be added to the Arras Memorial and a third in Tournai Cemetery.

The first was **Private Samuel Parker** 14841, 1st Bn., Royal Warwickshire Regiment, killed in action on the 3rd May, 1917. He was born and resided in Bedworth although he enlisted in Warwick. Samuel's name is recorded in 'Fallen Heroes' and on the Bedworth War Memorial. Reports of Samuel's service made the *'Bedworth and Foleshill News'* on September, 9th 1916 the article stated he had been *"wounded in the big push and now in hospital, formerly worked Newdigate Colliery, lived at the Woodlands. Been in France about six months since January, 1916. "*

The second name was **Corporal Michael Walker,** 10485, 5th Bn., Oxfordshire and Buckinghamshire Light Infantry. He was aged 24 and was the son of Mrs. Sarah Ann Jenkins of 11, Harold Street, Chilvers Coton, Nuneaton, the town where he also enlisted. He was born in Bedworth.

With a known grave, in Tournai Communal Cemetery Allied Extension, Belgium lies **Private William Gomm,** 33024, 1st Bn., Royal Berkshire Regiment, he was killed in action, 3rd May, 1917. A native of Banbury, he enlisted in Nuneaton and resided at 27, Wood Street, Collycroft, Bedworth. William's name is recorded in 'Fallen Heroes' and on the Bedworth War Memorial.

His official date of death is given as the 3rd May but local papers reported him as wounded on the 29th April, 1917 and no further news being heard by relatives, appeals were still being made by the family on the 15th June, 1917. As Tournai was held by the Germans until just before the Armistice and Allied prisoners of war were cared for locally, William may have been treated for wounds between the 29th April and the 3rd May. After the Armistice other graves were brought inform the surrounding area.

On the 4th May, 1917 **Private William Thomas Johnson**, 15355, 2nd Bn., Royal Warwickshire Regiment was killed. A native of Bedworth he also resided in the town and enlisted in Nuneaton. His name is recorded in 'Fallen Heroes' and on the Bedworth War Memorial. With no known grave he is commemorated on the Arras Memorial.

Private Joseph Allton, 22397, 15th Bn., Royal Warwickshire Regiment was the second son lost by Thomas and Maria Allton, of 14, Woodlands Road, Bedworth. Joseph (pictured right) was killed in action on the 8th May, 1917 aged 25. His brother was Private William Allton. Joseph was born on the 21st June, 1892 at Bedworth and resided with his parents. Joseph was employed as a Cycle Mechanic at Coventry Challenge Cycle Works Ltd until enlisting in October, 1916 at Warwick, he had been on active service since January, 1917. With no known grave, he is commemorated on the Arras Memorial and like his brother his name is recorded in 'Fallen Heroes' and on the Bedworth War Memorial.

An attack was planned for the 8th May with the objective being Fresnoy village however the attack was cancelled but during troop movement six other ranks were killed and eighteen wounded. The attack was planned for 2.00am on the 9th.

The 9th May saw another two Bedworth men killed, Private Samuel Pratt would ultimately be added to the Arras Memorial and Private Charles Reynolds died of wounds and was buried in Feuchy British Cemetery. Both men are recorded in 'Fallen Heroes' and on the Bedworth War Memorial. **Private Samuel Pratt**, 12636, 15th Bn., Royal Warwickshire Regiment, was aged 19 and the son of Arthur and Prudence Pratt of 59, Wood Street, Collycroft. He enlisted in Nuneaton and was born and resided in Bedworth. **Private Charles Reynolds**, 35023, 5th Bn., Royal Berkshire Regiment was born in Coventry, enlisted in Warwick and resided in Bedworth. Private Reynolds is one of 209 burials at Feuchy Cemetery and his grave had to be moved in 1926 to allow the construction of a railway station.

The attack happened as planned for the 15th Battalion, however the creeping barrage proved very slow and the troops were pinched between the enemy's barrage and the pace of their own cover, heavy casualties resulted. Although some troops managed to get near the objective a withdrawal was ordered. A roll count showed 7 other ranks killed, wounded 137 and 50 missing.

Lance Corporal Walter Smith, 4480, 1st Bn., Royal Warwickshire Regiment was killed in action on the 10th May, 1917 and is buried in Crump Trench British Cemetery, France which was made by fighting units between April and August 1917. Walter a resident of Coventry, a native of Bedworth and enlisted in Nuneaton.

Dying of wounds in the region of Etaples on the 12th May, 1917 was **Private Joseph Gatcliff Gilbert**, 20369, 11th Bn., Royal Warwickshire Regiment. He was aged 23 and the husband of C. B. Gilbert, of Black Bank, Bedworth where he was also born. One of the men who enlisted in Coventry, his name is recorded in 'Fallen Heroes' and on the Bedworth War Memorial. Private Gilbert is buried in Etaples Military Cemetery which is the largest in France at 10,773 casualties.

Originally reported as missing since the 16th May, 1917 was **Acting Sergeant Thomas Henry Lucas**, 11410, 6th Bn., King's Own Yorkshire Light Infantry. Thomas, age 27 was the son of James and Annie Lucas, 19, Walton Terrace, Newtown Road, Bedworth. Thomas was married to Olive Lucas of 14, Daisy Vale Terrace, Thorpe, Wakefield. A native of Bedworth, he enlisted in his wife's home town and his name is recorded in 'Fallen Heroes' and on the Bedworth War Memorial. With no known grave he is commemorated on the Arras Memorial.

From April to June, 1917, No.21 Casualty Clearing Station was at Nesle, and the dead from it were buried in a plot in Nesle Communal Cemetery. **Sergeant Patrick Cannon**, 20617, 14th Bn., Gloucestershire Regiment died of wounds on the 24th May, 1917. He was not a local as he was born in Bermondsey, London but must have moved to the area as he enlisted in Coventry. His name is recorded in 'Fallen Heroes' and on the Bedworth War Memorial.

The last casualty in May, 1917 was **Private Joseph Tallis**, 36471, 2nd Bn., Worcestershire Regiment who was listed as killed in action on the 27th May, 1917. Aged 26, he was married to Ethel Tallis, of 209, Bulkington Road, Bedworth and his parents, Joseph and Sarah Ann Tallis also resided at Bedworth. Joseph enlisted in Bedworth and his name is recorded in 'Fallen Heroes' and on the Bedworth War Memorial. He is one of the original burials in Croisilles British Cemetery, France.

One Bedworth man was killed in action in June, 1917 on the 14th , **Private Herbert Harris.** His service number was S/11010 and he served with "B" Coy. 1st Bn., Gordon Highlanders formerly 9th (Queen's Royal) Lancers. Herbert, aged 21, was the son of Henry and Annie Harris, of 82, Bulkington Lane, Bedworth. Born in Chilvers Coton, he enlisted in

Bristol and his name is recorded locally in 'Fallen Heroes' and on the Bedworth War Memorial. Private Harris is commemorated on the Arras Memorial.

On the 4th July 1917, **Private Frank Vincent Banwell**, 29702, 6th Bn., South Wales Borderers was killed in action and buried in Belgian Battery Corner Cemetery. This was named after the position of a Belgian artillery position and started after the Battle of Messines. Frank was the son of John and Susannah Banwell of Newport, Monmouthshire and born close by in Llantarnam, Monmouthshire. Although a resident of Bedworth, he enlisted in Llandilo, Carmarthen.

Rifleman Edward Tyler, R/7140, 2nd Bn., King's Royal Rifle Corps died of wounds on the 10th July, 1917 and was probably buried at night in Coxyde Military Cemetery. As the town was within shelling distance, burials from the front were carried out under the cover of darkness. Rifleman Tyler was aged 22 and the son of John and Hannah Tyler, of Woodland Villa, Woodlands, Bedworth. He was born and resided in Bedworth and enlisted in Nuneaton. Edward's name is recorded in 'Fallen Heroes' and the Bedworth War Memorial.

Brandhoek Military Cemetery contains 669 First World War burials and one of these is Bedworth man, **Driver Aubrey Harry Shillcock**, 113330, "B" Bty. 177th Bde., Royal Field Artillery. Aubrey was killed in action on the 19th July, 1917 and was one of the last burials in Brandhoek Military Cemetery before the use of a new cemetery. Aubrey, aged 18 was born in Black Bank to Arthur and Emma Elizabeth Shillcock. Aubrey enlisted in Coventry and is commemorated on the Exhall Memorial.

Corporal Clay Richards, 9880, 11th Bn., Royal Warwickshire Regiment died of wounds on the 26th July, 1917 and was buried in Locre Hospice Cemetery, Belgium probably after receiving treatment at the field ambulances which were stationed in the Convent of St. Antoine. He enlisted in Nuneaton, and as a resident of Bedworth his name is recorded in 'Fallen Heroes' and on the Bedworth War Memorial.

To commemorate the men who fell in the Third Battle of Ypres and have no known grave names would later be added to the Ypres (Menin Gate) Memorial, the first two Bedworth men who died on the 31st July, 1917.

Lance Sergeant Richard Raven, 7945, 1st Bn., Coldstream Guards was a native of Long Itchington, he enlisted in Warwick and resided in Stockton, Northamptonshire. Despite these locations his name is recorded in 'Fallen Heroes' and on the Bedworth War Memorial. In contrast, **Lance Corporal Samuel Harrison,** 18900, 7th Bn., Prince of Wales Volunteers (South Lancashire Regiment) was born in Bedworth and enlisted in Nuneaton and his name is recorded on the Bedworth War Memorial.

 Into August, 1917 and two Bedworth men were buried in the ironically named Mendinghem Military Cemetery, Belgium. The first was **Pioneer Amos Harry Courts**, 170795, A Special Coy., Royal Engineers who was killed on the 4th August, 1917 at the age of 28. Amos was married to Sarah Lillian Courts, of 65, Park Road, Bedworth and born in Longford. Although he resided at Coventry where he worked as a School Teacher he enlisted in London. Amos was also educated at Bablake School, Coventry and named after his father who was a coal miner. In addition to his name being recorded in 'Fallen Heroes' and on the Bedworth War Memorial he is also commemorated on the Education Department Memorial, Council House, Coventry Corporation and the Bablake School Memorial.

Three days later, **Private Thomas Martin,** 19254, 10th Bn., Royal Warwickshire Regiment was killed in action and with no known grave he is commemorated on the Ypres (Menin Gate) Memorial. Born and enlisted in Bedworth his name is recorded in 'Fallen Heroes' but not on the Bedworth War Memorial.

The second man buried in Mendinghem Military Cemetery is **Private Tom Bradbury**, 265158, D Coy., 1st/7th Bn., Royal Warwickshire Regiment who died of wounds on the 12th August, 1917 at the age of 22. Tom a native of Bedworth was the son of Joseph and Mary Ann Bradbury, of 2, Starkey's Yard, Leicester Road, Bedworth. Enlisting in Nuneaton his name is recorded in 'Fallen Heroes' and on the Bedworth War Memorial.

Also recorded locally both in Fallen Heroes' and on the War Memorial is **Private John Thomas Walker,** 41213, 1st Bn., Worcestershire Regiment who died of wounds on the 16th August, 1917. A native of Coventry, he resided and enlisted in Bedworth. On his death he was buried in Boulogne Eastern Cemetery, France which aligns with dying from wounds as this was one of the chief hospital areas.

 Two other Bedworth men would be killed in action on the 16th August, 1917. The first, aged 24, was **Company Sergeant Major William Goode**, 11309, Oxfordshire and Buckinghamshire Light Infantry. William was born in Exhall to Alfred W. Goode, of 5, Cleavers Yard, Bedworth and enlisted in Nuneaton. His name is recorded in 'Fallen Heroes' and on the Bedworth War Memorial, he is also the first Bedworth man commemorated on the Tyne Cot Memorial to 35,000 missing. Men who have no known grave after and including the 16th August, 1917 are named, the memorial is located at a site which marks the furthest point reached by Commonwealth forces in Belgium until nearly the end of the war.

The second was **Pioneer Albert Drakeford**. 130646, No. 1 Special Coy., Royal Engineers formerly 15232, Royal Warwickshire Regiment. Albert aged 20, mother was the son of Mrs. A. Drakeford, of 7, New Town Road, Bedworth. He was born and enlisted in Bedworth. Satisfying all criteria his name is recorded in 'Fallen Heroes' and on the Bedworth War Memorial. He is buried in Ramscappelle Road Military Cemetery, Belgium and his grave was probably brought in after the Armistice.

The same fate occurred to **Gunner Harry Dodd**, 840635, C Bty., 306th Bde., Royal Field Artillery who was killed on the 22nd August, 1917 at the age of 21. His grave is in Plot III, White House Cemetery significantly Plot I and II were completed during the war and Plot III were graves from battlefields around Ypres. He was named after his father, and his mother, Ada, resided at 138, Bulkington Road, Bedworth with her husband. Harry was a native of Bedworth and sought enlistment in Coventry. Harry's name is recorded in 'Fallen Heroes' and on the Bedworth War Memorial.

The men who fell with the Oxford and Buckinghamshire Light Infantry are commemorated on Panel 96 to 98 of the Tyne Cot Memorial and two Bedworth men fell on the 22nd August, 1917. **Private James Knibbs,** 10728, 2/4th Bn., was born in Bedworth, enlisted Nuneaton and resided in Foleshill. Perhaps for this reason he is not commemorated in Bedworth but his names appears on the Exhall Memorial and on Saint Thomas the Apostle Memorial in Longford.

In contrast**, Private William Jacques,** 240886, 2/1st Bn., Oxfordshire and Buckinghamshire Light Infantry formerly 6776, Norfolk Regiment has his name recorded in 'Fallen Heroes' and on the Bedworth War Memorial. William's father was also called William and he resided with his wife, Betsy at 10, Spencer Street, St. Albans. The youngest William was born and resided in Bedworth and enlisted in Coventry.

 **Private Joseph Edward Ludford** 11321, 5th Bn., Oxfordshire and Buckinghamshire Light Infantry was killed in action, the following day the 23rd August, 1917. He was born and enlisted in Nuneaton but resided in Bedworth with his name recorded in 'Fallen Heroes' and on the Bedworth War Memorial. Private Ludford rests in Tyne Cot Cemetery, his remains and Private Samuel Reynold's were added after the Armistice when the cemetery was enlarged with the dead of the surrounding battlefields.

Private Samuel Reynolds, 306801, 1/8th Bn., Royal Warwickshire Regiment was killed in action on the 27th August, 1917. He enlisted in Bedworth and his name is recorded in 'Fallen Heroes' and on the War Memorial.

Private Reynolds, memorial plaque, medals and scroll

The final casualty of August, 1917 on the 27th was **Corporal Thomas Charles Hammersley**, 268167, 2nd/7th Bn., Royal Warwickshire Regiment. Thomas was the son of David and Hannah Hammersley, of Bedworth and aged 22. He enlisted in Bedworth and his name is inscribed on the Bedworth War Memorial. Corporal Hammersley was buried in White House Cemetery.

With no known grave, **Private Walter Moore,** 203200, 2/5th Bn., Royal Warwickshire Regiment was killed on the 6th September, 1917 and is commemorated on the Tyne Cot Memorial. Walter, aged 39, was born in Bedworth to William and Maria Moore, who resided at Chilvers Coton, Nuneaton. He was the husband of Matilda Ellen Moore, of "Wilana," Long Shoot, Nuneaton and they resided at 508, Foleshill Road, Coventry. Walter enlisted in his wife's home town, Nuneaton. His photograph  appeared in *'The 'Coventry Herald'*, 12th October, 1917 with *'Private Walter Moore. Killed. 508 Foleshill Road'* .

 Reports were received that **Private Frederick William Vears**, 51909, 12th Sqdn., Machine Gun Corps (Cavalry) was killed by a shell on the 11th September 1917. A Native of Bedworth he was aged 21. His parents, Harry and Ellen Vears lived at various addresses the last known being 37, School Street, Bulkington; formerly they resided at Castle Inn and prior to this in Stockingford. Private Vears enlisted in Nuneaton and resided in Stockingford and was formerly employed in the 'Tunnel Pit' as a miner. During his service he was commended for bravery and his name is recorded in 'Fallen Heroes'. He is buried in Hargicourt British Cemetery which contains over 300 casualties.

In Plot I. C. 24. at Aeroplane Cemetery, Belgium lies the grave of **Private Wilfred Gledhill**, 241844, 1st/7th Bn., Lancashire Fusiliers. He died of wounds on the 13th September, 1917. The cemetery was original called New Cemetery, Frezenberg but as a crashed plane lay in the cemetery it quickly changed it's name. Wilfred was married to Florence Gledhill and he resided at 5, Sleath Yard, Bedworth. His parents, Mr. J. and Mrs. E. Gledhill, resided at 158, Oldham Road, Rochdale where he also enlisted. At the point of his death he was aged 23. He is locally commemorated in 'Fallen Heroes' and on the Bedworth War Memorial.

Commemorated on the Tyne Cot Memorial, in Fallen Heroes' and the Bedworth War Memorial is **Private James Atkins**, 15830, A Coy., 6th Bn., King's Own Scottish Borderers. At the age of 26, he was killed on the 23rd September, 1917. James's life locally was centred around Hartshill, Collycroft and Nuneaton. He was the son of William and Hannah Atkins of 328, Tuttle Hill, Nuneaton, the Husband of Florence May Felton (formerly Atkins) of 18, Royal Oak Yard, Collycroft, Nuneaton and was born in Hartshill. He also enlisted in Nuneaton.

Two Bedworth men died on the 24th September, 1917 and both are recorded in 'Fallen Heroes' and on the Bedworth War Memorial. **Private Harry Ashley Cooper**, 9797, 11th Bn., Royal Warwickshire Regiment was killed, aged 22. He was the son of Thomas Edward and Eliza Cooper, of 14, Rye Place, Bedworth, born in Bedworth and enlisted in Warwick. With no known grave he is commemorated on the Tyne Cot Memorial.

Dying of wounds on the 24th September, 1917 was **Sergeant George Arthur Cryer,** 12195, 6th Bn., Oxfordshire and Buckinghamshire Light Infantry, at the age of 37. George was the son of William and Eliza Cryer, of Bedworth. A native of Monks Kirby, he enlisted in Nuneaton and was a resident of Bedworth. Sergeant Cryer is buried in Dozinghem Military Cemetery. The 4th , 47th and 61st Casualty Clearing Stations were posted at Dozinghem and the military cemetery was used by them until early in 1918. This was one of a cluster of Clearing Stations ironically called Mendinghem, Dozinghem and Bandaghem.

Into October, 1917 on the 3rd and the 6th two Bedworth men would die of wounds and be buried in Godewaersvelde British Cemetery, France. They were probably treated at either the 37th, 41st or 11th casualty clearing stations as they were known to use this cemetery. **Private Walter Davis**, 19183, 1st Bn., South Staffordshire Regiment died of wounds on the 3rd. A native of Bedworth, he was the brother of Mrs. A.

Tudor, of 30, Police Row, Hamstead, Birmingham. He enlisted in Warwick and resided in Bedworth.

Private John Alfred Stevens, 7680, "B" Coy. 2nd Bn., Royal Warwickshire Regiment died on the 6th October, 1917 in the 37th Clearing Station, aged 22. John was named after his father and his mother was Emma Stevens, his parents resided at Woodlands Lane, Bedworth. John was born in Newtown, Leicester and enlisted at the age of 19 in September, 1914 at Rugby. Local reports show he had served in France for more then two years and was previously employed at Binley Colliery. John's name is recorded on the Bedworth War Memorial.

With no known graves, two Bedworth men who died on the 9th October , 1917 are commemorated on the Tyne Cot Memorial and recorded in 'Fallen Heroes' and on the Bedworth War Memorial. **Private David Phillips,** 24905, 22nd Bn., Machine Gun Corps (Infantry) formerly 11748, Royal Warwickshire Regiment was born in Stockingford, enlisted in Nuneaton and resided in Bedworth. The second was the most decorated casualty from Bedworth, **Corporal Thomas Brindley, DCM, MM.**

His service number, 4417, 2nd Bn., was with the Royal Warwickshire Regiment and he was born in Bedworth, enlisted in Nuneaton and resided in Chilvers Coton. Corporal Brindley was awarded the Military Medal and the Distinguished Conduct Medal for conspicuous gallantry and devotion to duty appearing in 'The London Gazette', 18th July, 1917: *"He made five journeys over exposed ground in order to gain information of the situation. This was carried out under heavy machine gun and rifle fire and finally he bought back one wounded officer".*

A third casualty on the 9th October, 1917 was **Private Sidney Niblett**, 21679, 2nd Bn., Royal Warwickshire Regiment who died of wounds, age 22. Sidney was married to Mrs. A. Cornish (formerly Niblett), of "Ivydean," 11, Coventry Road, Bedworth although he was born in

118

Dordon, Warwickshire. He enlisted in Nuneaton and his name is recorded in 'Fallen Heroes' and on the Bedworth War Memorial. Private Niblett is buried in Buttes New British Cemetery, Polygon Wood, Belgium and this was made after the Armistice with the dead from the battlefields of Zonnebeke. This cemetery contains 2,108 graves with 1,677 unidentified.

The following day, **Lance Corporal, George William Bodell**, 25496, 112th Coy., Machine Gun Corps (Infantry) formerly 4204, Royal Warwickshire Regiment died from wounds. He was born in Warwickshire and enlisted in Nuneaton with his name being recorded both in 'Fallen Heroes' and on the Bedworth War Memorial. On his death he was buried in Outtersteene Communal Cemetery Extension, France . After the Armistice, over 900 graves were brought into this cemetery from the battlefields surrounding Outtersteene and from smaller cemeteries.

On the 13th October, 1917 **Gunner Thomas Cole**, 163734, Y/ 9th Trench Mortar Bty., Royal Field Artillery was killed in action. He enlisted and resided in Bedworth and his name is duly recorded in 'Fallen Heroes' and on the Bedworth War Memorial. His grave is one of the 383 original burials in La Brique Military Cemetery No.2, Belgium that were made between February 1915 and March 1918.

Lance Corporal Henry Brough Till, 20527, 1st Bn., South Staffordshire Regiment is commemorated on the Tyne Cot Memorial to the missing. He was killed in action on the 26th October, 1917. Although he enlisted in Nuneaton and resided in Bedworth, Henry was a native of Gentleshaw, Staffordshire and born to Thomas and Caroline Jane Till, who later resided at 54, Leicester Road, Bedworth. Aged 26, his name is recorded in 'Fallen Heroes' and on the Bedworth War Memorial.

The last casualty of October, 1917 was **Lance Corporal, Isaac Fletcher**, 4477, 1st Bn., Royal Warwickshire Regiment who died of wounds on the 31st October, 1917 at the age of 31. Isaac was the son of William and Minnie Fletcher, of Bedworth and resided at 183, College Street,

Chilvers Coton, with his wife Beatrice Catharine Fletcher. A native of Collycroft, he enlisted locally in Nuneaton and his name is recorded in 'Fallen Heroes' and on the Bedworth War Memorial. Lance Corporal Fletcher is buried in Mont Huon Military Cemetery, Le Treport, Seine-Maritime, France. Le Treport became an important hospital centre and those that died in the hospitals were originally buried in Le Treport cemetery but as it reached capacity a new cemetery was required at Mont Huon.

Three Bedworth men died in November, 1917. The first was **Private, Norris William Bray**, T/242995, 3/4th Bn., Queens Regiment (Royal West Surrey Regiment) who died of wounds on the 9th November, 1917 at the age of 19. Norris was the son of Charles and Harriet Bray of Leire, Rugby, where he was also born. He later resided at Bedworth and enlisted in Nuneaton. Private Bray is recorded in 'Fallen Heroes' and on the Bedworth War Memorial and he is buried in Longuenesse (St. Omer) Souvenir Cemetery, France. St. Omer suffered from air raids in November, 1917 and it is possible that Norris was one of the victims, Casualty Clearing Stations were also based in the town during the war.

On the 17th November, 1917 the 148th Coy., Machine Gun Corps (Infantry) lost **Private John Thomas Clarke**, 114820, formerly 37710, Somerset Light Infantry when he was killed in action at the age of 25. John's mother, Matilda Clarke lived at 37, Roadway, Bedworth. He was born in Bedworth, enlisted in Nuneaton and resided in Bedworth. Being so local, his name is recorded in 'Fallen Heroes' and on the Bedworth War Memorial. With no known grave he is commemorated in the Tyne Cot Memorial.

The last casualties of November, 1917 and added to the Thiepval Memorial is **Private George Thomas Henson**, 23984, 5th Bn., South Wales Borderers who died on the 22nd November, 1917 at the age of 21. George was named after his father, George James Henson, who resided at 10, Chapil Street, Bedworth. George Thomas was born in Hinckley, Leicestershire, enlisted in Leicester and resided in Coventry.

Grave Ref. A. 26. Villiers Plouich Communal Cemetery, France marks the burial of **Private William George Burgess,** 202407, 2/4th Bn., Royal Berkshire Regiment who was killed on the 4th December, 1917. Villiers Plouich is a small cemetery with just over 50 casualties. Enlisting in Reading but a resident of Collycroft, William's name is recorded in 'Fallen Heroes' and on the Bedworth War Memorial.

Added after the Armistice added to Loos British Cemetery, was the grave of **Private William Brown,** 28216, 9th Bn., Sherwood Foresters, (Notts and Derby) Regiment who was killed in action on the 12th December, 1917. Graves were brought to Loos British Cemetery from small graveyards and the battlefields. William was born in Bedworth and enlisted in Mansfield. His name is recorded in 'Fallen Heroes' and on the Bedworth War Memorial.

The last two men who died in December, 1917 are commemorated on the Thiepval Memorial. **Private Peter Tyler,** 328043, 2nd /8th Bn., Royal Warwickshire Regiment was killed in action on the 15th December, 1917 aged 29. Peter's parents, William and Sarah resided at Bedworth Hill whilst records indicate Peter resided in Bedworth although he enlisted in Coventry. His name is commemorated on the Exhall Memorial.

Private John Norman Smith, 68072, 7th Bn., Royal Fusiliers formerly 7835, 2/5th Queen's Royal West Surrey Regiment was killed on the 30th December, 1917. A native of Bedworth, he enlisted and resided in Coventry.

1918

Into 1918 and three new memorials to the missing would be required. The Pozieres Memorial relates to March and April 1918 when the Allied Army was driven back by overwhelming numbers across the former Somme battlefields, and the months that followed before the Advance to Victory, which began on the 8th August 1918. The Memorial commemorates over 14,000 casualties who died on the Somme from 21st March to 7th August 1918. The Soissons Memorial commemorates almost 4,000 officers and men of the United Kingdom forces who died during the Battles of the Aisne and the Marne in 1918 and who have no known grave. This Memorial bears the names of over 9,000 men who fell from the 8th August 1918 who have no known grave.

The first death of 1918 has a known grave; **Private Samuel Felton**, DM2/097037, 51st Div. Supply Col., Motor Transport, Royal Army Service Corps died of wounds on the 29th January, 1918. He was born in Oldbury, Worcestershire and later moved to Bedworth although he enlisted in Birmingham. With his residence in Bedworth his name is recorded in 'Fallen Heroes' and on the Bedworth War Memorial. Private Felton is buried in Achiet-Le-Grand Communal Cemetery Extension, France which during the period of his death was being used by medical units in particular the 45th and 49th Casualty Clearing Stations.

The first Bedworth man to be commemorated on the Pozieres Memorial is **Private Oliver Thomas Smith**, 16441, 15th Entrenching Bn., previously 11th Bn., Royal Warwickshire Regiment who died of wounds on the 22nd March, 1918 at the age of 24. Oliver's parents were John Oliver and Agnes Smith, of The Post Office, Bulkington and he was born on the 30th July, 1894 at Bulkington. He was one of the twenty three casualties who enlisted in Bedworth, which he did in February, 1916. Oliver was employed as a carpenter and the '*City*

of Coventry Roll of the Fallen' suggests he was possibly buried near St. Quentin.

Also dying of wounds, two days later, was **Private George Noel Phillips**, 12986, 10th Bn., Royal Warwickshire Regiment formerly 3529, Life Guards, aged 28. George was married to Ann Sarah Phillips, of 66, Marston Lane, Collycroft, Bedworth and his parents, Leonard and Hannah Phillips resided in Bedworth. George was born in Stockingford, and enlisted in Coventry. His name is recorded in 'Fallen Heroes' and on the Bedworth War Memorial. Private Phillips is one of 676 men buried in St. Pierre Cemetery, France; at the time of his death this was being used by the 41st and 42nd Stationary Hospitals.

With no known grave is **Pioneer Charles Herbert Rowe**, 130645, 1st Special Coy., Royal Engineers formerly Royal Warwickshire Regiment, who was killed on the 24th March, 1918, aged 21 and commemorated on the Pozieres Memorial. Charles was born on the 14th July, 1896 at Leicester to Thomas Arthur and Edith Rowe, who later resided at 124, Coventry Road, Bedworth. Until enlisting in November, 1915 he worked as a labourer. His name is recorded in 'Fallen Heroes' and on the Bedworth War Memorial.

In the Arras sector, with his name recorded on the Arras Memorial was **Private Ernest Arthur Fowkes**, PLY/2313, 1st R. M. Bn., Royal Marine Light Infantry who was also killed on the 24th March, 1918. Ernest's name is recorded in 'Fallen Heroes' and on the Bedworth War Memorial.

After the war, Corporal Callent of Coventry who was Ernest who reached home as a released prisoner said *"Private Fowkes was hit in the chest by a bullet from a German sniper at about 9.00am on Palm Sunday, 24th March. There was just time before the company were all taken prisoners to bind him up and place him on a stretcher when they were compelled to leave him, as his Corporal is convinced to a dying condition."* The local papers reported; *"as nothing further has been heard of him, it may unfortunately be assumed*

123

that the wound proved fatal. Well known. He was a sidesman of the Parish Church, Superintendent Collycroft Sunday School, and a devoted church worker".

The third man commemorated on the Pozieres Memorial is **Private, Charles Jacques**, (served as Smith), 10128, 5th Bn., Northamptonshire Regiment who was killed on the 27th March, 1918, aged 33. Charles was named after his father who resided at 13, Queen Street, Bedworth. Private Jacques is recorded on the Bedworth War Memorial.

 The last death of March 1918 was **Lance Corporal Thomas Harrison**, 266445, 2nd/7th Bn., Royal Warwickshire Regiment was killed in action on the 30th March, 1918 at the age of 21. Thomas's parents were Alfred and Rosa Harrison, of 6, Roadway, Bedworth and he was born and resided in Bedworth although he enlisted in Coventry. Private Harrison is recorded in 'Fallen Heroes' and on the Bedworth War Memorial and commemorated on the Pozieres Memorial. A series of letters he send home poignantly ended with the words, *"Kiss Ethel for me."*

The Pozieres Memorial is also the place of remembrance for **Lance Sergeant Henry Marston,** 242469, 2/6th Bn., Royal Warwickshire Regiment who was killed on the 3rd April, 1918. A native of Lubenham, Leicestershire, he enlisted in Nuneaton and resided in Foleshill, Coventry. Despite no obvious connection to Bedworth his name is recorded in 'Fallen Heroes'.

Private William H. Bray, 11368, 2nd Bn., Oxfordshire and Buckinghamshire Light Infantry died of wounds on the 6th April, 1918. at the age of 24. His parents were Thomas Henry and Mary Ann Bray, of 124, Bulkington Road, Bedworth. William was born and resided in Bedworth and enlisted in Nuneaton. With a strong Bedworth connection his name is recorded in 'Fallen Heroes' and on the Bedworth War Memorial. As Private Bray is buried in Etaples Military Cemetery, he would have been treated in a hospital in the vicinity prior to his death.

Military Medal winner, **Corporal John Bagnall Jones MM,** 65147, 105th Field Coy., Royal Engineers was killed on the 11th April, 1918. A native of Bedworth he enlisted further afield in Marylebone, Middlesex closer to his mother, Mrs. Sophia Jones of 12, Howley Place, Paddington, London. With no known grave Corporal Bagnall is commemorated on the Arras Memorial.

 Three days later saw the loss of **Private Fred A. Akerman**, 12350, 2nd Bn., Irish Guards. He was aged 35 and the husband of Elsie Wilson (formerly Akerman), of Beech House, Saunders Avenue, Bedworth. Fred was born in Loughborough, enlisted in Coventry and was a resident of Bedworth and his name is recorded in 'Fallen Heroes' and on the Bedworth War Memorial. The 'Bedworth and Foleshill News' reported; "News received by his wife, killed in action during the big German attacks. He had only been in the army three or four months, aged 34. Fred was one of the principal workers at the local Wesleyan church and Sunday school and it was noted a tribunal had ordered him to join up".

The tribunal had taken place in July, 1916 as his previous hearing had been adjourned. Fred argued that "he supplied every article in the home and since making the claim he had lost his father and the maintenance of his mother would now fall upon him. He was allowed one month to make arrangements and during this time was to give up some of his time to work of national importance." With no known grave he is commemorated on an Addenda Panel on the Ploegsteert Memorial.

The 15th April, 1918 brought the death of **Private Edmund Saunders**, 28714, 1st Bn., Royal Warwickshire Regiment who was killed in action aged 33. Edmund was the son of Harry and Sarah Saunders and the husband of Elsie Ann Saunders of 51, Titford Road, Langley,

Birmingham. He was born at Leamington, enlisted in Bedworth and his name is recorded in 'Fallen Heroes'. Private Saunders is buried in Grave Ref. IV. D. 35. Choques Military Cemetery, France.

Two men would either be killed or action or die of wounds on April, 17th and they are the last deaths in April. **Private Thomas William Lydster**, 41928, 2nd Bn., Worcestershire Regiment was killed in action, aged 19. He was named after his father and his mother Mary, resided with her husband at Bedworth Heath. Thomas was born and resided in Bedworth and enlisted in Nuneaton. He is named on the Bedworth War Memorial and recorded in 'Fallen Heroes'. His final commemoration is on the Ploegsteert Memorial.

Dying of wounds, on the 17th April was **Corporal Thomas Brown**, 37532, 18th Bn., Northumberland Fusiliers. Although he was born in Bedworth, he enlisted in Derby. The Bedworth War Memorial bears his name as does 'Fallen Heroes'. Corporal Brown is buried in Mendinghem Military Cemetery and would have been treated at one of the Casualty Clearing Stations close by.

Two Bedworth men died in May, 1918 and both are commemorated in 'Fallen Heroes' and on the Bedworth War Memorial. The first was **Private Thomas Johnson,** 34232, 1st Bn., Gloucestershire Regiment who died on the 8th May, 1918. A native of Bedworth, he enlisted in Warwick. Private Johnson is buried in St. Hilaire Cemetery Extension, Frevent, France; the majority of the burials in the cemetery were carried out from the 6th Stationary Hospital hospitals, the 3rd Canadian, and the 19th and 43rd Casualty Clearing Stations. Frevent was a place of importance on the lines of communication during the First World War.

126

 Two days later, **Private Fred Charles Cotton**, 28322, 1st Bn., Royal Warwickshire Regiment formerly 27354, Hussars was killed in action. He was born in St. Pancras, Middlesex and enlisted in London so his association with Bedworth is due to his working locally, his name is recorded in 'Fallen Heroes' and on the Bedworth War Memorial. After the Armistice, graves were brought in from the battlefields immediately east of the village of Hinges and Private Cotton was probably amongst them as he is buried in Hinges Military Cemetery.

His death was covered in the *'Bedworth and Foleshill News'*, 11th September, 1918: *"Before enlisting Private Cotton worked at Messrs. Stanley's Charity Pit, Bedworth. He came from a soldierly family, two brothers being on active service. Private Cotton's Father also served in the Royal Staffordshire Regiment. He enlisted when he was 17 and had been at the front since the outbreak of hostilities. His ancestors were involved in the Battle of Waterloo and his parents stated he was always a good son to them."*

One Bedworth death was recorded in June 1918. **Private Ernest William Wright**, 42434, 2nd Bn., Royal Berkshire Regiment who was killed on the 11th June, 1918. He was born and resided in Bedworth and enlisted in Nuneaton. Private Wright's name is recorded in 'Fallen Heroes' and on the Bedworth War Memorial. He is the first Bedworth man commemorated on the Soissons Memorial.

Buried in St. Amand British Cemetery, France is **Lance Corporal Robert Frank Harris,** S/32358, 13th Bn., Rifle Brigade formerly M/288349, Royal Army Service Corps who was killed on the 4th August, 1918 at the age of 19. He was the son of John and Elizabeth Harris, of "Roseville," Dugdale Street, Nuneaton where he enlisted although he was born in Bedworth. St. Amand Cemetery was used particularly by the 37th and the 56th (London) Divisions in August 1918, in total there are over 200 casualties.

The second death in August 1918 was **Private Walter George Albert Tudge**, 7th Bn., T/206327, Queen's Royal West Surrey Regiment formerly 22835, Royal Warwickshire Regiment who died of wounds on the 23rd August, 1918. Walter enlisted in Warwick with his original unit the Royal Warwicks and he resided in Bedworth. His name is recorded in 'Fallen Heroes' and on the Bedworth War Memorial. Private Tudge is buried in Daours Communal Cemetery Extension, France; the area around the cemetery was almost a front line up to the middle of August and towards the end of the month was used by a number of Casualty Clearing Stations based near Daours. In September the cemetery was closed.

The 15th Bn., King's Own (Yorkshire Light Infantry) lost **Private Charles John Gillam**, service number 64665 formerly 30178, Gloucestershire Regiment who was killed in action on the 27th August, 1918. Charles was the son of John and Alice Gillam and died age 33. He was the husband of Ann Maria Gillam of 56, Duns Tew, Deddington, Oxford and was born in Acton, Middlesex and enlisted in Nuneaton. Private Gillam's name is recorded in 'Fallen Heroes' and on the Bedworth War Memorial and he is buried in Outtersteene Communal Cemetery Extension, Bailleul, France.

With no known grave, **Rifleman, Samuel Henry Wills**, 880616, 34th Bn., London Regiment formerly 36928, Devonshire Regiment is commemorated on the Loos Memorial. He was killed in action on the 2nd September, 1918, he started life in Bedworth and enlisted in Nuneaton.

The following day, the 3rd September, **Able Seaman Able Broadbent**, R/3684, Hawke Bn. R.N. Div., Royal Naval Volunteer Reserve died at the age of 29. Able was the son of James and Naomi Broadbent of 32, Croft Road, Bedworth Heath. He was the husband of Elsie Broadbent and is recorded in 'Fallen Heroes' and on the Bedworth War Memorial. Able Seaman Broadbent is buried in Queant Road Cemetery, Buissy, France; this was reached on the 2nd September 1918, and evacuated by the Germans on the following day. Although the dates align, his burial in this cemetery was made after the Armistice.

 Formerly Service No. 39377, Royal Warwickshire Regiment, **Private Thomas Robert Haynes,** died as Service No. 28931 with the 15th (Hampshire Yeomanry) Bn., Hampshire Regiment on the 4th September, 1918 at the age of 18. He was the son of John and Emma Haynes', of 47, Roadway, Bedworth and enlisted in Nuneaton. Private Haynes name is recorded in 'Fallen Heroes' and on the Bedworth War Memorial. His grave was made after the Armistice, when graves were brought in from isolated sites and smaller cemeteries to replace the French graves (of April and September 1918) that were removed to a French cemetery; many of the men re-interned were of the 15th Hampshires who recaptured the ground near the cemetery in September 1918.

With his name inscribed on the Vis-en-Artois Memorial is **Private Walter Smith,** 24120, 15th Bn., Royal Warwickshire Regiment who was killed in action on the 27th September, 1918 at the age of 20. Walter was the son of Mrs. Mockford of 27, Hazlewood, Terrace, Collycroft, Nuneaton and born in Collycroft. He possibly resided with his mother in Collycroft and enlisted in Nuneaton.

Also killed in action on the 27th was **Private Donald Grant Neale,** 95332, 15th Bn., Tank Corps formerly 4259, Royal Warwickshire Regiment. A native of Chilvers Coton, he enlisted in Nuneaton and has his name recorded in 'Fallen Heroes' and on the Bedworth War Memorial. Donald is one of 565 burials in Moeuvres Communal Cemetery Extension, France; the extension was made between September and October 1918 and enlarged after the Armistice.

Private Albert Knight, 94080, 1st Bn., King's Liverpool Regiment formerly 37756, Royal Warwickshire Regiment died of wounds on the 29th September, 1918. A resident of Bedworth, he was also born in the town and enlisted in Coventry with his name recorded in 'Fallen Heroes'. Private Knight is buried in Grevillers British Cemetery, France; at this point various Casualty Clearing Stations were in the region and using the cemetery although after the Armistice, 200 graves were brought in from the battlefields to the south of the village.

Targelle Ravine British Cemetery was made in September and October, 1918. With over a 100 casualties many of them belonged to the 9th Highland Light Infantry (Glasgow Highlanders). One of the burials is **Private John T. Harvey**, 242571 formerly 10923, Leicestershire Regiment who was killed on the 29th September, 1918. John was born in Featherstone, Yorkshire and must have moved to the Bedworth area, enlisting in Nuneaton and residing in Bedworth. His name is recorded in 'Fallen Heroes' and the Bedworth War Memorial.

The third death on the 29th September, 1918 was **Private Henry Burks**, 16183, 1st Bn., Duke of Cornwall's Light Infantry. Henry was born in Bedworth, enlisted in Warwick and resided in Leamington Spa. He is buried in Grave Ref. II. D. 12. Fifteen Ravine British Cemetery, Villiers Plouich, France and his grave was brought in after the Armistice.

Two Bedworth men were killed in action on the 9th October, 1918 and they are both recorded in 'Fallen Heroes' and on the Bedworth War Memorial and lie in Busigny Communal Cemetery Extension, France. Both were re-interned after the Armistice from smaller cemeteries although the actual village was captured by the 30th American Division and British cavalry on this day. The first was **Private George Brindley**, 42357, 1st/5th Bn., Gloucestershire Regiment formerly 42104, Royal Berkshire Regiment. He was born in Bedworth and enlisted in Warwick. **Private Albert Farndon**, 42356, 1/5th Bn., Gloucestershire Regiment formerly 42710, Royal Berkshire Regiment was born in Bedworth and enlisted in Nuneaton.

After the Armistice it was reported that **Acting Sergeant Tom Twigger,** 139210, 250th Tunnelling Coy., Royal Engineers formerly 11367, Oxfordshire and Buckinghamshire Light Infantry was instantly killed with two comrades removing a mine on the 16th October, 1918. He was aged 24 and the son of Sarah Twigger, of 7, Foster's Yard, Roadway, Bedworth and was also born in the town. Tom

enlisted in Nuneaton, with his name recorded in 'Fallen Heroes' and on the Bedworth War Memorial. He is buried in Grave Ref. IV. A. 3. La Gorgue Communal Cemetery, France.

Less then a week later, **Private Joseph John Lakin,** 32106, 1st Bn., Duke of Cornwall's Light Infantry formerly 3897, 92nd T. Res. Battalion died of wounds on the 22nd October, 1918. With his name recorded in 'Fallen Heroes' and the Bedworth War Memorial, research shows he was born in Bedworth and enlisted in Nuneaton. Joseph is buried in Rocquigny-Equancourt Road British Cemetery, France and this was in use by the 3rd Canadian and 18th Casualty Clearing Stations in October, 1918.

The 23rd to the 24th October, Pommercuil was the scene of severe fighting and the cemetery was made after the capture of the village. Pommereuil British Cemetery contains 173 burials, one of whom is **Private Harry Palmer,** 57199, 1st/8th Bn., Royal Warwickshire Regiment who was killed on the 23rd. Harry was the son of Henry and Martha Palmer, of 47, Heath Road, Bedworth and aged just 19 at the point of his death. He was born in Bedworth, enlisted in Nuneaton and resided in Collycroft, Bedworth. Private Palmer's name is recorded in 'Fallen Heroes' and the Bedworth War Memorial and he is buried in Pommereuil British Cemetery, France.

'The Battalion War Diary' notes: " *The attack commenced at 01.20am the Battalion moving in rear of the 9th Devons and the Battalion was to be used to*

131

mop up Pommereuil if necessary or if this necessity did not arise to pass through the 7th Brigade and carry the intermediate objective. Owing to heavy fog the attacking units of the first wave became rather mixed up and the situation was for sometime obscure but on Captain H. Mortimore going out and taking command of the troops of all units and organising attacks on enemy machine gun nests which had been missed by the first wave owing to the fog, the situation rapidly cleared and all objectives were gained."

Also recorded in 'Fallen Heroes' and on the Bedworth War Memorial is **Private Amos William Jacques**, 41769, 1st Bn., Royal Warwickshire Regiment who was killed on the 24th October, 1918. Amos was born and resided in Bedworth and enlisted in Leamington. He is buried in Verchain British Cemetery, France which was used for a total of one week from the 24th October to the 1st November and has over 100 burials.

By the end of the day, the 1st Battalion recorded 95 casualties killed or missing. *'The Battalion War Diary'* records "*Zero hour was at 04.00am and our own artillery was a little short to begin with causing casualties. Verchain was entered with large numbers of the enemy giving themselves up, the high ground North East of Verchain encountered a trench line and machine guns with further advance rendered impossible at this time.*"

 **Rifleman Leonard Henry Chatwin**, R/42175, King's Royal Rifle Corps posted to London Regiment (Queen Victoria Rifles) formerly TR/9/25267, 45th T. R. Battalion died of wounds on the 27th October, 1918 at the age of 18. He was the son of Henry J. and Elizabeth Chatwin, of 4, Queen Street, Bedworth and born in the town. Enlisting in Nuneaton his name is recorded in 'Fallen Heroes' and on the Bedworth War Memorial. He resided at Whitehouse, Coventry Road, Bedworth and is buried in Arras Road Cemetery, Roclincourt, France. This cemetery was enlarged in 1926-29, with the addition of 993 graves from the areas mainly North and East of Arras.

Graves were also brought into St. Aubert British Cemetery, France after the Armistice where **Private Walter Henry Smith**, 42742, 14th Bn., Royal Warwickshire Regiment is buried. He died on the 29th October, 1918 at the age of 26. Walter was married to Ada Sturges Smith of 6, Melton Street, Kettering and was born in Kenilworth although he enlisted in Bedworth. Private Smith's name is recorded in 'Fallen Heroes' and on the Bedworth War Memorial.

The first of two casualties in November, 1918 was killed on the 1st November, 1918. **Private Albert John Knight**, 43395, "A" Coy. 2nd/8th Bn., Worcestershire Regiment. Aged 19, he was the son of Arthur and Sarah Knight, of 251, Bulkington Road, Bedworth and was also born in the town. He enlisted in Nuneaton and resided in Bedworth with his name recorded in 'Fallen Heroes' and on the Bedworth War Memorial. Private Knight's grave in Cross Roads Cemetery was added after the Armistice.

The last death prior to the Armistice was **Private James Ivor Meyrick**, 57351, 10th Bn., Royal Warwickshire Regiment who died of wounds on the 8th November, 1918, aged 21. James was born in Foleshill to Walter Henry and Katherine Meyrick who later resided at Bedworth. He enlisted in Coventry and resided in Bedworth, with his name recorded in 'Fallen Heroes' and on the Bedworth War Memorial. He is one of the original burials in Awoingt British Cemetery, France and these were made by the 38th, 45th and 59th Casualty Clearing Stations. On the 8th November the Battalion were involved in an attack to the East of Malplaquet and were held up by machine gun fire.

The last burial in the Western Front was **Private Thomas. H. Daffern**, 310476, 18th Bn., Tank Corps who died on the 17th December, 1918 at the age of 21. Thomas was the son of Joseph and Sarah Daffern, of 8, Heath Villas, Bedworth and his name is recorded on the Bedworth War Memorial. On his death he was buried in St. Pol British Cemetery, St. Pol-Sur-Ternoise, Pas de Calais, France, with the cemetery used by No. 12 Stationary Hospital.

Unverified

From the Bedworth War Memorial and the 'Our Boys' Book a number of names were found that could not be verified with the Commonwealth War Grave Commission, 'Soldiers Died in the Great War' database or a search of the Medal Index Cards. Men who were discharged from service are not included with the Commonwealth War Grave Commission, men who died after 1919 are not included on Soldiers Died in the Great War and some of the Medal Index Card are missing or filed incorrectly. The latter only shows information relevant to medal entitlement and not information on date of death etc.

The first name in alphabetical order is **S. Biddle,** who is referred to in 'Fallen Heroes' as attached to the Worcestershire Regiment. There is one medal index card for a Samuel Biddle, 27828 Worcestershire Regiment formerly 533430 Labour Corps and one death listed with the Commission for a Samuel Arthur Biddle 2nd Bn., Royal Berkshire Regiment who died age 18 on the 1st July, 1916 in the Battle of the Somme.

With his name recorded in 'Fallen Heroes' and on the Bedworth War Memorial is **Ernest Blake,** Royal Fusiliers. No matching details could be found with the Commission, two men named Ernest Blake served with the Fusiliers but no deaths were recorded. Named on the Bedworth War Memorial is **Henry Butlin.** Only one Henry Butlin is listed with the Commission a Sir Henry Guy Trentham Butlin who fell on the 16th September, 1916 with the Cambridgeshire Regiment. The National Archives show six medal index cards with the most likely candidate being Private, 17932 Royal Warwickshire Regiment.

Daffern, N. J., Tank Corps is included in 'Fallen Heroes'. No matches could be found with the Tank Corps however the *'Bedworth and Foleshill News'* dated 29th May, 1916 in the list of wounded included a N. Daffern, 12138 Royal Warwickshire, of Bedworth. The Medal Index

Card shows he was formerly Private, 48552 with the Leicestershire Regiment.

Recorded in 'Fallen Heroes' and the Bedworth War Memorial is **Samuel Freemantle**, Royal Warwickshire Regiment. No matches could be found for a Medal Index Card and the Commission lists two Samuel Freemantles neither of whom were in the Royal Warwickshire Regiment.

Also with his name recorded in 'Fallen Heroes' and the Bedworth War Memorial is a **Private Harry Gee,** Oxfordshire and Buckinghamshire Light Infantry. No matches could be found with the Commission and a Private John H. Gee, 30247 served with the Oxfordshire and Buckinghamshire Light Infantry and these details are also listed under men who served. A Lieutenant Harold Gee formerly a Private with the Notts and Derby Regiment moved to the Oxfordshire and Buckinghamshire Light Infantry. Also with the Oxford and Bucks is **Thos. Griffiths** who's name is recorded in 'Fallen Heroes'. No matching details could be found with the Commission but a Private, 12176 served with the 6th Battalion.

Having his name recorded in 'Fallen Heroes' and on the Bedworth War Memorial is **Thomas Jones**, Royal Naval Division. There were thirty two men who served with the Royal Naval Division who match there criteria so the exact one could not be ascertained.

Kemp, John T. Royal Warwickshire Regiment is recorded in 'Fallen Heroes'. No match could be found with the Commission and thirty men with the surname Kemp served with the Royal Warwickshire Regiment, one died who was J. E. 10th Bn. Royal Warwickshire who died on the 5th September, 1918.

More elusive is **Knight, Alfred** who is recorded on the Bedworth War Memorial, there are two hundred and twenty seven men who served matching the criteria of Alfred Knight.

With his name recorded in 'Fallen Heroes' is **Martin, D.**, Royal Berkshire Regiment, no matches could be found and matched these criteria. Recorded in 'Fallen Heroes' is Ernest Rowe, Royal Warwickshire Regiment. Two Ernest Rowe's died with the Royal Warwickshire Regiment, the first died with the 1st Bn., on the 25th October, 1916 and with the 2/8th Bn., the second Ernest Rowe died on the 1st July, 1916.

The War Memorial records a **Patrick Musson.** A P. Musson, G/36660 served with the Royal West Kent Regiment and died on the 8th September, 1918. He is buried in St. Sever Cemetery Extension, Rouen, France.

The name of **Saunders, Ernest** is recorded on the Bedworth War Memorial although it is possible this was meant to be Edmund who died on active service. No matches could be found fully matching this criteria, the Commission shows 82, E. Saunders with 176 Medal Index Cards. A **Smith, W. A.**, Royal Engineers is recorded in 'Fallen Heroes' and a **Smith, Walter** named on the Bedworth War Memorial.

Recorded in 'Fallen Heroes' is **Stokes, J.**, Northamptonshire Regiment: no matches could be found and it is possible that this was a duplicate entry for John Thomas Stokes. The other, **Stokes, W. F.**, Royal Warwickshire Regiment is recorded in 'Fallen Heroes'. A William David Stokes died on the 23rd July, 1916, aged 24 and a Private William F Stokes, 2661, has a Medal Index Card. No matches could be found for **Tallis, Samuel,** Oxfordshire and Buckinghamshire Light Infantry who has his name recorded in 'Fallen Heroes' and on the Bedworth War Memorial.

There is no Medal Index Card or match with the Commission. **Tibbits, W.**, Royal Fusiliers is recorded in 'Fallen Heroes', no matches could be found with the Commission and a total of nine Medal Index Cards matched the criteria of W. Tibbitts with an extra T. One in particular, Walter Tibbitts, 15433, Royal Fusiliers, formerly G/92986, Middlesex Regiment.

The final man is **Watts, John. W.** whose name is recorded on the Bedworth War Memorial. There are six matches with the Commission but none show a reference to Bedworth. This is possibly Private Walter John Smith, 266520, 1/7th Bn., Royal Warwickshire Regiment who was killed in action on the 13th August, 1917. He was born on 29th December, 1887 at Coventry where he was employed as a labourer prior to the outbreak of war.

Honour the Servicemen

'The Coventry Graphic' reported on the 26th September, 1919 under the headline 'Ex-Service Men Honoured' and sub headline 'Bedworth's Splendid Programme;' "That the parishioners of Bedworth are to be congratulated on the splendid welcome home they gave to 850 heroes on Saturday. The town rose to the occasion and an appeal for subscription realised about £500, which included £50 from Messrs. Courtauld's Ltd. The tradesmen and residents put out their flags in profusion and from one end to another the town was a mass of colour.

A perambulation of the chief streets opened the programme, the men walking four-a-breast accompanied by members of the committee and the Leicester Military and Bedworth Town Bands. On reaching Mr. Cleaver's field in the Coventry Road, dinner was served in a spacious marquee. When the 850 men were seated they presented a fine spectacle, the decorations of the table being an elaborate scale. Mr. W. H. Alexander (Chairman of the Committee) offered grace, in the absence of Canon F. R. Evans (Rector). The guests were waited upon by eighty ladies assisted by a number of men and forty boy scouts.

At the conclusion of the repast an interesting ceremony took place from the bandstand i.e the distribution of decorations won on the battlefield by local men. Mr. Alexander was chairman, and he was supported by Canon Evans, Major and Mrs. Orton, Major Wood, the Reverends W. D. Rudgard, W. Pugh and J. F. Bradley, Father Wall, Mr. W. Johnson, Mr. G. Pickering, Mrs. E. W. Orton, Mr. J. Daffern, Mr. A. H. Lawrence, Mr. and Mrs. J. Downing etc. apologies for absence were announced from the Earl of Denbigh, Colonel Wyley, Lieutenant Fitzroy, Mrs. Quick, Mr. H. Maddocks M. P., Councillor W. H. Grant, Mr. E. Wootton, Rev. S. C. Waldegrave, Mr. Johnson (Courtaulds), etc. The names of the men were called out by Mr. A. H. Lawrence and then Canon Evans pinned the decorations on the breasts of the recipients.

Complimentary and congratulatory speeches were delivered by the Chairman, Canon Evans, Major Orton and Mr. W. Johnson and Mr. Lawrence returned thanks on behalf of the men. Sports were carried through, the prize money (£60) being distributed by Mr. H. J. Edmands (Tower House). A Punch and Judy show, variety artistes and concerts by the Leicester Military Band were much enjoyed and the Bedworth Band played for dancing. A splendid display of fireworks and a big bonfire brought a comprehensive programme to a termination. The committee and hon. Secs (Messrs. W. Johnson and H. J. Edmands) are to be heartily complimented upon the success of the event. The large picture shows the interior of the marquee, with the men assembled for dinner; the other one Canon Evans distributing the war decorations. Inset Mr. Elliott the caterer and Mr. H. J. Edmands one of the hon. secretaries.

Honours List

Deceased

Corporal Tom Brindley. DCM, MM.	*Royal Warwickshire*
Bombardier George Henry Dean. MM	*Royal Field Artillery*
Lance Corporal William Joseph Priest. DCM, MM	*Royal Field Artillery*

Private J. Beddows. MM	Gloucestershire Regiment
Sergeant George Bennett. DCM, MM	Royal Field Artillery
Gunner Fred. A. Bosworth. MM	Royal Field Artillery
Sapper Thomas Bucknall. DCM	Royal Engineers
Gunner Thomas Bucknall. MM	Royal Garrison Artillery
Captain W. Carding. MC	South African Infantry
Private W. Carvell. MM	Oxfords and Bucks Infantry
Private A. Cluley. MM	London Regiment
Second Lieutenant A. Croxall. MM	Oxfords and Bucks Infantry
Gunner W. Daffern, W. MM	Royal Field Artillery
Sapper J. B. Dunkley, C. de G	Royal Engineers
Bombardier Joseph Farndon. MM.	Royal Field Artillery
Gunner , Erskine Gibberd. MM	Royal Field Artillery
Bert Howe. MM	Royal Field Artillery
Driver H. Howe. MM	Royal Army Service Corps
Sergeant John Leach. MM.	Royal Warwickshire
Private F. J. Lucas. MM	Royal West Kent Regiment
Private Edgar Meyrick. MM	Royal Warwickshire
Private G. Mountford. MM	Royal Field Artillery
Private Bertie E. Parsons. MM	Worcestershire Regiment
Sergeant Isaac Randle. MM	Royal Field Artillery
Sergeant Lionel Randle. MM with Bar	Kings Royal Rifle Corps
Sergeant Leon W.Shortridge. DCM, MM	Royal Engineers
Sergeant T.Tallis. MM	Royal Warwickshire
Private Jack Walker. MM	Royal Warwickshire
Sergeant Whelan. MM	Irish Fusiliers
Private Whyman. MM	Royal Warwickshire

War Memorial

On the 12th July, 1918 the Editorial of ' *The Coventry Graphic'* provoked the following under the headline *'War Memorials';* "*Bedworth Parish Council has been discussing the subject of a permanent war memorial, and in this connection a free library, baths, and public park or recreation ground were mentioned. There is always an abundance of enterprise and enthusiasm on the part of Bedworth people, but it is hoped they will not be carried away in that respect. Before either scheme could be safely entered upon, at least £2,000 – that is putting it at the very lowest – would have to be guaranteed, and whichever suggestion found favour there would be the maintenance and upkeep to be considered.*

We know the promoters of any memorial scheme would look for financial assistance from outside, but the fact must not be overlooked that probably each individual parish will have it's own war memorial sooner or later. At the meeting to which we refer the Councillors themselves were by no means unanimous as to which of the three schemes were preferable. An argument in favour of a free library was that it would be a splendid place for young people in the winter evenings; another member favoured baths, seeing that Bedworth was a colliery district; and yet another opinion was distinctly favourable to a public park or recreation.

When Bedworth did possess a recreation ground nine out of every ten of the juvenile population preferred to disport themselves on the highway. The suggestion has been thrown out that Bedworth and Exhall, as neighbouring parishes should amalgamate for the purposes of a war memorial and go in for a public park at a certain point. We could imagine Bedworth adults and juveniles walking a mile or more to a park or recreation ground! We think the Parish Council were well advised in allowing the matter to stand over till such time it was opportune to ask a parish meeting to consider a proposal".

As the discussion on the subject of war memorials developed the editorial of *'The Coventry Graphic'* on the 23rd May, 1919 was again quite vocal stating: *'In various parishes adjacent to Coventry during the present week, public meetings have been held to consider the question of Peace memorials, but we are sorry to say that in several instances there were meagre attendances and little enthusiasm was aroused. We have all long been of an opinion that this is not the time or occasion for 'boisterous' festivities and instead of spending huge sums in that manner, it would be far preferable to devote the money to permanent memorials which would be of lasting good to the community.*

The rates are heavy enough and public authorities should hesitate before taking money from the sources for festivities. Neither should they embark on memorials which would entail an expensive up keep. The dependents of the men who have fallen and the heroes who have returned are the people who should have the first consideration in whatever is attempted, and war memorials ought to take the form of something that would be of real benefit to them. Public parks or open spaces find a lot of favour, and in this respect Coventry has set a commendable example which might with advantages be followed by Foleshill and Bedworth, who are so far undecided as to the shape their war memorials will take.

The Unveiling
Unveiling Bedworth's War Memorial

'*The Coventry Graphic*' on the 21st January, 1921 reported the dedication of Bedworth's War Memorial. The Rev. Canon F. R. Evans, M. A. Rector of Bedworth and Rural Dean, unveiled the Bedworth War Memorial on Sunday afternoon in the presence of several thousand spectators. Fortunately the threatened rain kept off, and the proceedings were most impressive. The memorial takes the form of a massive monument in the cemetery, and has been erected at the cost of some hundreds of pounds, the principle subscribers being Messrs. Courtaulds Ltd., of Coventry, a considerable portion of whose labour is drawn from Bedworth and district.

The memorial was erected from designs by Major H. C. Corlette of London. It is built of Hollington stone, on a base taking the form of a cross, supporting a square shaft on the sides of which are inscribed the names of the 205 men who laid down their lives in the war, surmounted by a spire rising to a height of 21ft. The monument bears the following inscription "*In Honoured Memory of the Bedworth men who fell in the Great War, this monument is erected by their fellow parishioners and friends, A. D. 1920*".

These men of ours, unselfish, unafraid
Went to the world-wide light
Forget not how they fought and how we prayed
For England and for right.

The members and officials of Bedworth Parish Council attended the ceremony in their official capacity, and some hundreds of ex-servicemen many of them wearing their medals – walked in procession to the cemetery, headed by a band of music. A space around the monument was roped off for the accommodation of the ex-servicemen, Parish Council officials, relatives and friends of the deceased. The proceedings opened with the beautiful hymn "O, God our help in ages past", The Rev. J. F Bradley read sentences from the Scriptures and Canon Evans offered prayers. The last named unveiled the monument and dedicated it in the following sentences :" *In the name of the Father and of the Son, and of the Holy Ghost we dedicate this monument erected by their fellow townspeople and friends to the honoured and lasting memory of men who died for their country and for the cause of right and liberty in the world. May the good God bless our deed. May the remembrance of a splendid effort and noble self-sacrifice inspire us to concentrate our lives unselfishly to the promotion amongst all men, all nations, of righteousness, fellowship, goodwill and peace".*

Addressing the large gathering Canon Evans expressed the opinion that it was a ceremony in which they had the sympathy of the parishioners generally and said it was a proud privilege to unveil such a memorial. It had been set up as an expression of the honour, respect and gratitude which they felt for those who had fought for their country in time of need, so many of whom gave their lives in the cause. It was a grave crisis at the time – the question of whether might should prevail over right – and these men came forward and fought for the side they believed to be right. No one could do more than to be faithful to what he believed to be his duty, "even unto death," or die more honourably than in such a cause as those men fought for. They had on the monument the names of 205 Bedworth men who made the last sacrifice for their country and for us, and they had erected the monument as a sign of their (the parishioners') pride and thankfulness for the bravery and unselfish devotion to duty.

It was as enduring a monument as man knew how to raise. Canon Evans also paid a tribute to the men who had served and returned and remarked upon the debt which we owed them for their services. He thought we should do all in our power to help them to recover the positions they forfeited when they gave up in order to serve.

Mr. A. H. Lawrence also spoke briefly at the invitation of the ex-service men, remarking that they were most grateful to Canon Evans for his sympathetic and inspiring address. He (Mr. Lawrence), appealed to one and all to display that spirit of comradeship which the soldiers had done, and prove that they were not unmindful of the great sacrifices they had made, especially by those whose memory they were honouring that day, and who had fought so that others may live. The "Last Post" having been sounded, relatives and others filed by the monument to deposit wreaths etc. There were probably over 100 of these floral tributes, including those of the ex-soldiers, Parish Council, Bedworth Brotherhood, political and Working Men's Club etc.

Bedworth Armistice Day Parade

Following the War Memorial dedication, in 1921 a local school teacher and Great War veteran, Alfred Lawrence organised the first Armistice Day Parade. After his invaluable service the role of organising fell to Tom Bucknall who was also a Great War veteran. After the Second World War the task fell to a local business man and war veteran, Maurice Smart.

In 1986, Frank Parsons (pictured) an ex-Royal Marine Commando and World War Two veteran took responsibility for organising the parade. The parade focuses around the War Memorial although the parade route has had to accommodate changes to the town and the number of attendees.

The fundamental role of the parade is to honour those who fell in both wars and remembering those who have died in conflicts since 1945. The salute is taken by the Lord Lieutenant of Warwickshire, The Mayor of Nuneaton and Bedworth, the MP for Bedworth and North Warwickshire, the MP for Nuneaton and high ranking officers.

The parade draws over 5,000 people to the town as the tradition is maintained of having the event at the exact day, month and time of the the effect of the Armistice came into place. The document was signed at 5.00am by Allied Supreme Commander Ferdinand Foch's and a German delegation in Foch's railway carriage with a six hour effect window.

The Armistice originally ran for 30 days, being renewed until a formal peace treaty was signed at Versailles in 1919. The carriage was to be used again when Hitler made France sign an Armsitice on German terms in the same carriage.

Conclusion

Throughout the Great War the citizens of Bedworth applied themselves to the war effort, over 1,200 men would serve with the colours and over a further 200 would make the 'Supreme Sacrifice'. With their roots in a mining community, these skills were utilised and many of the men went on to serve with Tunnelling Companies of the Royal Engineers.

At home to underpin the war effort, coal still needed to be extracted and miners risked challenges on a daily basis. Although belated, the award of an Edward Medal to John Johnson for an act of bravery in July, 1915 at Newdigate Colliery pays testimony to this and the working conditions endured by the miners in this period. The close proximity to Coventry would have seen many of the men and women employed in munitions work at various factories.

The formation of the 'Our Boys' Fund saw to it that those serving were not forgotten and appeals for funds were met admirably. The compilation of names in the 'Our Boys' Booklet in 1919 has aided research considerably. As this was published prior to the dedication of the War Memorial in 1921, it has highlighted that the names of the fallen differ. There are a possible number of reasons for this and the use of modern databases has highlighted that a number of names could be added to the War Memorial at a future date. Bedworth was represented in many of the major battles throughout the war and the names of those who fell appear on headstones and memorials throughout France, Belgium, Turkey, Iraq, Greece, Iran and Egypt.

Less then twenty years after the War Memorials dedication the citizens of Bedworth were called upon with the outbreak of the Second World War. The unique tradition of maintaining the Armistice Parade from 1921 and throughout the Second World War has ensured that Bedworth is synonomous with commemoration on a national and international level.

Alphabetical Roll of the Fallen

AKERMAN, Private, Fred A.	14th April, 1918
ALLEN, Corporal, William John.	16th July, 1916
ALLTON, Private, Joseph.	8th May, 1917
ALLTON, Private, William.	21st June, 1916
ARNOLD, Private, Charles Sidney.	11th February, 1917
ATKINS, Private, James.	23rd September, 1917
AUSTIN, Corporal, Lawrence.	12th July, 1916
AYRES, Lnc Cpl, George William.	23rd June, 1917
BAILEY, Private, Ernest John.	5th July, 1916
BAILEY, Private, John.	25th March, 1916
BANWELL, Private, Frank Vincent.	*4th July, 1917*
BARLOW, Private, John.	3rd September, 1916
BARTLETT, Bombardier, William.	*8th June, 1915.*
BATES, Private, Harold.	19th July, 1916.
BEASLEY, Private, Joseph.	29th October, 1915.
BERRILL, Sapper, George. W.	23rd September, 1919.
BIDDLE, Private, Frank.	3rd September, 1916.
BIDDLE, S.	
BIRD, Lance Corporal, James.	*13th March, 1917.*
BLAKE, Ernest.	
BODELL, Lnc Cpl, George William.	10th October, 1917.
BOWERS, Private, George.	30th July, 1916.
BOWNS, Private, Thomas Henry.	5th July, 1917.
BRADBURY, Private, Tom.	12th August, 1917.
BRAMLEY, Corporal, Thomas.	10th April, 1917.
BRAY, Private, Norris William.	9th November, 1917.
BRAY, Private, William H.	6th April, 1918.
BRINDLEY, Private, George.	9th October, 1918.
BRINDLEY, Cpl, Thomas, DCM, MM.	9th October, 1917.
BROADBENT, Able Seaman, Able.	3rd September, 1918.
BROWN, Corporal, Thomas.	17th April, 1918.
BROWN, Private, William.	12th December, 1917.

BUCKNALL, Private, Thomas. 9th May, 1917.

BURGESS, Private, William George. 4th December, 1917.

BURKS, Private, Henry. *29th September, 1918.*

BUTLER, Private, Harry. 11th April, 1917.

BUTLIN, Henry.

CANNON, Sergeant, Patrick. 24th May, 1917.

CARTER, Private, Herbert Harry. 28th April, 1917.

CARTER, Private, Walter Harry. 25th January, 1917.

CARVELL, Driver, Ernest Edward. 9th December, 1918.

CASSELL, Private, John. 25th April, 1915.

CATER, Private, Edgar Percival. 24th August 1916.

CHATWIN, Rifleman, Leonard Henry. 27th October, 1918.

CLARKE, Private, John Thomas. 17th November, 1917.

COLE, Gunner, Thomas. 13th October, 1917.

CONWAY, Private, George. *14th July, 1915.*

COOPER, Private, Harry Ashley. 24th September, 1917.

COPE, Sergeant , Walter. 26th October, 1915.

COTTON, Private, Fred Charles. 10th May, 1918.

COURTS, Pioneer, Amos Harry. 4th August, 1917.

CRUTCHLOW, Private, Arthur. 16th January, 1917.

CRUTCHLOW, Stoker, 1st Class, David. 12th January, 1918.

CRUTCHLOW, Private, Herman. 15th July, 1916.

CRYER, Sergeant, George Arthur. 24th September, 1917.

DAFFERN, N. J.

DAFFERN, Private, Thomas. H. 17th December, 1918.

DARLISON, Private, Thomas. 15th June, 1918.

DAVENPORT, Private, Sam. 4th December, 1917.

DAVIS, Private, Walter. *3rd October, 1917.*

DEAN, Bdr, George Henry, MM. 4th September, 1916.

DERICOTT, Private, Thomas. 15th June, 1918.

DODD, Gunner, Harry. 22nd August, 1917.

DRAKEFORD, Pioneer, Albert. 16th August, 1917.

EDMANDS, John. 25th April, 1915

EDWARDS, Private, Benjamin. 21st April, 1917.

EDWARDS, John Thomas	16th June, 1918.
EDWARDS Private, John.	6th August, 1915.
EVERITT, Private, Harry.	18th August, 1916.
FARNDON, Private, Albert.	9th October, 1918.
FARNDON, Private, Herbert A.	20th March, 1916.
FATHERS, Gnr, Frederick William.	8th February, 1916.
FELTON, Private, Samuel.	29th January, 1918.
FLETCHER, Lance Corporal, Isaac.	31st October, 1917.
FORD, Private, Edward, A.	25th January, 1917.
FOWKES, Private, Ernest Arthur.	24th March, 1918.
FOX, Sapper, Frederick Beauclerc.	31st August, 1915.
FREEMAN, Second Lieutenant, Tom.	17th February, 1917.
FREEMANTLE, Samuel.	
FRISWELL, Private, John Padbury.	16th May, 1915.
FULLYLOVE, Private, John.	25th April, 1917.
GAMMAGE, Lce Cpl, Albert	13th August, 1916
GEE, Private, Harry.	
GIBBERD, Private, Arthur Stanley.	7th July, 1915.
GIBBS, Private Alfred.	*14th July, 1916.*
GILBERT, Private, Joseph Gatcliff.	12th May, 1917.
GILLAM, Private, Charles John.	27th August, 1918.
GLEDHILL, Private, Wilfred.	13th September, 1917.
GOMM, Private, William.	3rd May, 1917.
GOODE, Private, Charles Henry.	3rd September, 1916.
GOODE, CSM, William.	16th August, 1917.
GRIFFIN, Private, Arthur.	9th October, 1916.
GRIFFIN, Private, Walter.	9th May, 1916.
GRIFFITH, Private, Arthur.	4th September, 1916.
GRIFFITHS, Thos.	
HALL, Private, Charles.	26th April, 1915.
HAMMERSLEY, Private, Arthur.	25th January, 1917.
HAMMERSLEY, Cpl Thomas	27th August, 1917.
HARDIMAN, Gnr, Thomas George.	21st October, 1916.
HARRIS, Private, Herbert.	14th June, 1917.

HARRIS, Lnce Cpl, Robert Frank.	4th August, 1918.
HARRISON, Lnce Cpl, Samuel.	31st July, 1917.
HARRISON, Lnce Cpl, Thomas.	30th March, 1918.
HARRISON, Private, William.	16th July, 1916.
HARTOPP, Gman, Harry Edward.	14th April, 1916.
HARVEY, Private, John T.	29th September, 1918.
HARVEY, Walter.	2nd April, 1918.
HASTINGS, Private, William George.	22nd November, 1916.
HAYNES, Private, Thomas Robert.	4th September, 1918.
HAYWOOD, Private, Jesse.	25th September, 1915.
HENSON, Private, George Thomas.	22nd November, 1917.
HENTON, Private, Joseph.	25th September, 1915.
HEWITT, Rifleman, Arthur Edward.	27th September, 1916.
HILL, Private, John Thomas.	15th July, 1916.
HILL, Private, Rowland William.	18th November, 1916
HOBBS, Private, Frank Alfred.	25th September, 1915.
HOBBS, Lance Corporal, John Allen.	9th July, 1916.
HORNER, Private, Charles Frederick	28th April, 1917.
HUNT, Lance Corporal, Stanley Albert.	25th September, 1915.
JACQUES, Private, Amos William.	24th October, 1918.
JACQUES, Private, Charles	27th March, 1918.
JACQUES, Private, George Thomas.	3rd October, 1915.
JACQUES, Private, Thomas.	22nd October, 1915.
JACQUES, Private, William.	22nd August, 1917.
JACQUES, Acting Corporal, William.	4th October, 1916
JEE, Sapper, Harry.	20th August, 1915.
JOHNSON, Private, John.	9th September, 1918.
JOHNSON, Private, Peter.	30th October, 1914.
JOHNSON, Private, Thomas.	8th May, 1918.
JOHNSON, Private, William Thomas.	4th May, 1917.
JONES, Corporal, John Bagnall, MM.	11th April, 1918.
JONES, Able Seaman, Robert	9th July, 1917.
JONES, Thomas.	
ISON, Private, Charles Albert.	22nd December, 1914.

KEMP, Private, George Thos.	3rd September, 1916.
KEMP, John T.	
KIMBERLEY, Private, Reuben.	1st July, 1916.
KNIBBS, Private, James.	*22nd August, 1917.*
KNIGHT, Private, Albert.	*29th September, 1918.*
KNIGHT, Private, Albert John.	1st November, 1918.
KNIGHT, Alfred.	
KNIGHT, Private, John.	16th July, 1916.
LAKIN, Private, Joseph John.	22nd October, 1918.
LEACH, Private, Bert.	20th October, 1915.
LEACH, Private, Isaac.	15th June, 1915.
LENTON, Private, Charles Joseph.	9th August, 1916.
LOLE, Private, Harry.	*26th January, 1917.*
LONG, Private, Joseph.	10th August, 1915.
LOVETT, Private, Leonard.	6th August, 1915.
LUCAS, Able Seaman, Richard Bert	*11th March, 1915.*
LUCAS, Sergeant, Thomas Henry.	16th May, 1917
LUDFORD, Private, Joseph Edward.	23rd August, 1917.
LUDGATE, Lance Corporal, Joseph.	11th July, 1915.
LYDSTER, Private, Thomas William.	17th April, 1918.
MALLABONE, Lce Cpl, Thomas.	*12th March, 1916.*
MARPLES, Private, Henry.	20th February, 1918.
MARSTON, Lnce Sgt, Henry.	3rd April, 1918.
MARSTON, Lance Corporal, Thomas.	1st September, 1916.
MARTIN, Private, Alfred.	3rd September, 1916.
MARTIN, Private, Benjamin.	6th April, 1916.
MARTIN, D.	
MARTIN, Private, Thomas.	7th August, 1917.
MEYRICK, Private, James Ivor.	8th November, 1918.
MIDDLETON, Gunner, Alfred George.	*27th August 1916.*
MILLS, Private, Sydney Ernest.	*2nd May 1915.*
MONTGOMERY, Charles Paul.	24th October, 1916.
MOORE, Private, Joseph.	24th August, 1916.
MOORE, Private, Thomas.	*8th December, 1916.*

MOORE, *Private, Walter.*	*6th September, 1917.*
MOORE, *Private, William.*	*3rd September, 1916.*
MOORE, Private, William Alfred.	26th September, 1916.
MORSON, *Corporal, Cyril*	*15th July, 1916*
MORSON, Walter.	7th August, 1916.
MUSSON, *Private, Ernest.*	*27th August, 1916.*
NEALE, Private, Alexander Grant.	19th July, 1916.
NEALE, Private, Donald Grant.	27th September, 1918.
NIBLETT, Private, Sidney.	9th October, 1917.
NICHOLLS, Private, William.	11th March, 1916.
PAGE, Corporal, Cyril Morson, MM.	15th July, 1916.
PAGE, Private, Harry.	21st January, 1919.
PALMER, Private, Harry.	23rd October, 1918.
PARKER, Private, Samuel.	3rd May, 1917.
PARSONS, AM 3rd Cl, Ernest. R. F.	21st October, 1918.
PARSONS, Private, Victor Reginald.	30th May 1917.
PAYNE, *Private, Ernest.*	*30th January, 1917.*
PEGG, *Private, Thomas.*	*3rd September, 1916.*
PENN, Private, Harry.	17th February, 1918.
PHILLIPS, Private, David.	9th October, 1917.
PHILLIPS, Private, George Noel.	24th March, 1918.
PICKARD, Private, Oliver.	25th September, 1915.
PICKER, Private, Frederick.	12th December, 1916.
PIPER, Private, Albert Charles.	20th March, 1916.
PRATT, Private, Samuel.	9th May, 1917.
PRIEST, Lce Cpl, William Joseph, MM.	29th January, 1917.
PULLIN, *Sapper, Frank.*	*19th July, 1916.*
RALLEY, Private, Abram.	11th June, 1915.
RANDLE, *Private, George. T.*	*31st August, 1916.*
RANDLE, *Private, Joseph.*	*1st July, 1916.*
RANDLE, Private, Levi.	13th March, 1915.
RAVEN, Lance Sergeant, Richard.	31st July, 1917.
REYNOLDS, Private, Charles.	9th May, 1917.
REYNOLDS, Private, James.	11th November, 1918.
REYNOLDS, Private, Samuel.	27th August, 1917.

RICHARDS, Corporal, Clay. 26th July, 1917.

RICHARDS, Guardsman, Harry. 14th September, 1916.

RIDER, Private, Joseph. 10th April, 1917.

ROBINSON, Corporal, William. *25th May, 1919*

ROWE, Pioneer, Charles Herbert. 24th March, 1918.

ROWE, E.

ROWLAND, Private, Samuel. 14th February, 1916.

ROWLEY, Private, William H. 13th October, 1914.

RUSH, Private, Robert Henry. 25th September, 1915.

SAUNDERS, Private, Edmund. *15th April, 1918.*

SAUNDERS, Ernest.

SEDGWICK, Rifleman, Joseph. 6th July, 1915.

SHARPE, Private, Israel. *7th August, 1915.*

SHILLCOCK, Driver, Aubrey Harry. *19th July, 1917.*

SKINNER, Private, William Matthew. 17th November, 1916.

SMALLEY, Private, Thomas. 10th March, 1915.

SMITH, Private, Arthur. 29th August, 1916.

SMITH, Private, John Norman. *30th December, 1917.*

SMITH, Private, Oliver Thomas. *22nd March, 1918,*

SMITH, W. A.

SMITH, Private, Walter. 27th September, 1918.

SMITH, Walter.

SMITH, Lance Corporal, Walter. 10th May, 1917.

SMITH, Private, Walter Henry. 29th October, 1918.

SMITH, Private, William. 13th August, 1916.

SMITH, Private, William Ernest. 5th October, 1918.

SPACEY, Private, John William. 9th September, 1916.

SPARROW, Private, Frederick. 11th April, 1917.

SPEDING, Private, Tom. 18th August, 1915.

SPENCER, John. Arnold. 15th September, 1916.

SPENCER, Private, John Thomas. 5th February, 1917.

SPENCER, Private, Samuel. 24th October, 1914

STEVENS, Private, John Alfred. 6th October, 1917

STOKES, J.

STOKES, Private, John Thomas.   30th November 1914.

STOKES, Lce Cpl, William Henry.   16th June, 1915.

STOKES, W. F.

TALLIS, Private, Joseph,   27th May, 1917.

TALLIS, Samuel.

TALLIS, Private, Thomas.   19th July, 1916.

TALLIS, Lance Corporal, William.   15th February, 1917.

TALLIS, Acting Corporal, William A. 5th October, 1918.

THORPE, Private, Richard.   13th August, 1916.

TIBBITTS, Private, Jack Abraham.   25th September, 1915

TIBBITS, W.

TIDMAN, Private, Thomas.   24th August, 1916.

TILL, Lance Corporal, Henry Brough. 26th October, 1917.

TOPP, Private, Aubrey   *19th July, 1916*

TREADWELL, Private, George.   19th May, 1916.

TUDGE, Private, Walter George Albert. 23rd August, 1918.

TWIGGER, Private, Amos.   17th April, 1917.

TWIGGER, Private, Ernest.   5th August, 1915.

TWIGGER, Acting Sergeant, Tom.   16th October, 1918.

TYLER, Rifleman, Edward.   10th July, 1917.

TYLER, Private, Peter.   *15th December 1917.*

VEARS, Private, Frederick William.   *11th September 1917.*

WALKER, Private, John Thomas.   16th August, 1917.

WALKER, Corporal, Michael.   *3rd May, 1917.*

WALKER, Private, Thomas.   3rd June, 1915.

WALKER, Private, Thomas William. 2nd July, 1916.

WATTS, John. W.

WHITCROFT, Private, Tom.   19th July, 1916.

WILKINS, Private, George Samuel.   *3rd September, 1916.*

WILLS, Rifleman, Samuel Henry.   *2nd September, 1918.*

WILSON, Private, Roland.   *12th October, 1916.*

WORTHINGTON, Gunner, William. 24 July 1916.

WRIGHT, Private, Ernest William.   11th June, 1918.

Geographical Roll of the Fallen

Belgium

Aeroplane Cemetery, Ieper, West-Vlaanderen
GLEDHILL, Private, Wilfred. Grave Ref. I. C. 24.

Belgian Battery Corner Cemetery
BANWELL, Private, Frank Vincent. Grave Ref. I. C. 18.

Berks Cemetery Extension
MONTGOMERY, Charles Paul. Grave Ref. I. I. 1.

Brandhoek Military Cemetery, Ieper, West-Vlaanderen
SHILLCOCK, Driver, Aubrey Harry. Grave Ref. I. M. 35.

Buttes New British Cemetery, Polygon Wood, Zonnebeke, West-Vlaanderen
NIBLETT, Private, Sidney. Grave Ref. I. C. 20.

Coxyde Military Cemetery, Koksijde, West-Vlaanderen
TYLER, Rifleman, Edward. Grave Ref. I. D. 49.

Dozinghem Military Cemetery, Poperinge, West-Vlaanderen
CRYER, Sergeant, George Arthur. Grave Ref. VIII. D. 20.

Dranoutre Military Cemetery
MARSTON, Lance Corporal, Thomas. Grave Ref. I. H. 2.

La Brique Military Cemetery No.2,
COLE, Gunner, Thomas. Grave Ref. I. K. 1.

Lijssenthoek Military Cemetery
PIPER, Private, Albert Charles. Grave Ref. V. D. 8A.

Locre Hospice Cemetery
RICHARDS, Corporal, Clay. Grave Ref. I. B. 4.

Mendinghem Military Cemetery, Poperinge, West-Vlaanderen.
BRADBURY, Private, Tom. Grave Ref. IV. B. 51.
COURTS, Pioneer, Amos Harry Grave Ref. IV. A. 5.

Menin Road South Military Cemetery
HARTOPP, Guardsman, Harry Edward. Grave Ref. I. J. 18.

Ploegsteert Memorial, Comines-Warneton, Hainaut
AKERMAN, Private, Fred A. Addenda Panel.
LYDSTER, Private, Thomas William. Panel 5.
PICKARD, Private, Oliver. Panel 7.

Potijze Burial Ground Cemetery
TREADWELL, Private, George. Grave Ref. A. 11.
Ramscappelle Road Military Cemetery, Nieuwpoort, West-Vlaanderen,
DRAKEFORD, Pioneer, Albert. Grave Ref. II. B. 10.
Tournai Communal Cemetery Allied Extension
GOMM, Private, William.   Grave Ref. V. A. 15.
Tyne Cot Cemetery
LUDFORD, Private, Joseph Edward.   Grave Ref.XLVIII.C. 11
REYNOLDS, Private, Samuel.   Grave Ref. IX. B. 9.
Tyne Cot Memorial Zonnebeke, West-Vlaanderen
ATKINS, Private, James.   Panel 66 to 68
BRINDLEY, Corporal, T, DCM, MM.   Panel 23,28 and 163A
CLARKE, Private, John Thomas.   Panel 154, 159 and 163A.
COOPER, Private, Harry Ashley.   Panel 23, 28 and 163A.
GOODE, CSM, Major, William. Panel 96 to 98.
JACQUES, Private, William.   Panel 96 to 98.
KNIBBS, Private, James.   Panel 96 to 98
MOORE, Private, Walter.   Panel 23, 28 and 163A.
PHILLIPS, Private, David.   Panel 154, 159 and 163A.
TILL, Lance Corporal, Henry Brough. Panel 90, 92, 162, 162A.
Voormezeele Enclosures No 1 and No,2, Ieper, West-Vlaanderen
NICHOLLS, Private, William.   Grave Ref. I. C. 21.
Voormezeele Enclosure No.3, Ieper, West-Vlaanderen
HAYNES, Private, Thomas Robert.   Grave Ref. XVI. L. 17.
White House Cemetery, St. Jean-Les-Ypres, Ieper, West-Vlaanderen
DODD, Gunner, Harry.   Grave Ref. III. G. 16.
HAMMERSLEY, Cpl, Thomas Charles. Grave Ref. II. A. 13.
Ypres (Menin Gate) Memorial, Ieper, West-Vlaanderen
CASSELL, Private, John.   Panel 8.
HALL, Private, Charles.   Panel 8.
HARRISON, Lance Corporal, Samuel. Panel 37.
HENTON, Private, Joseph.   Panel 37 and 39.
JOHNSON, Private, Peter.   Panel 22.
LUDGATE, Lance Corporal, Joseph. Panel 37 and 39.
MARTIN, Private, Thomas.   Panel 8.
MILLS, Private, Sydney Ernest.   Panel 8.

RAVEN, Lance Sergeant, Richard.   Panel 11.

RUSH, Private, Robert Henry.   Panel 52.

SEDGWICK, Rifleman, Joseph.   Panel 51 and 53.

SPENCER, Private, Samuel.   Panel 8.

STOKES, Private, John Thomas.   Panel 43 and 45.

STOKES, Lce Cpl, William Henry.   Panel 34.

WALKER, Private, Thomas.   Panel 8.

Egypt

Alexandria (Chatby) Military and War Memorial Cemetery

JACQUES, Private, George Thomas.   Grave Ref. D. 146.

Alexandria (Hadra) War Memorial Cemetery

CARVELL, Driver, Ernest Edward.   Grave Ref. H. 9.

France

Achiet-Le-Grand Communal Cemetery Extension

FELTON, Private, Samuel.   Grave Ref. II. E. 13.

Albert Communal Cemetery Extension, France.

BEASLEY, Private, Joseph.   Grave Ref. I. A. 13.

Arras Memorial

ALLTON, Private, Joseph.   Bay 3.

BRAMLEY, Corporal, Thomas.   Bay 3.

CARTER, Private, Herbert Harry.   Bay 3.

EDWARDS, Private, Benjamin.   Bay 8.

FOWKES, Private, Ernest Arthur.   Bay 1.

HARRIS, Private, Herbert.   Bay 8 and 9.

HORNER, Private, Charles Frederick.   Bay 2 and 3.

JOHNSON, Private, William Thomas.   Bay 3.

JONES, Corporal, John Bagnall, MM.   Bay 1.

LUCAS, Acting Sgt, Thomas Henry.   Bay 7.

PARKER, Private, Samuel.   Bay 3.

PRATT, Private, Samuel.   Bay 3.

RIDER, Private, Joseph.   Bay 3.

TWIGGER, Private, Amos.   Bay 3.

WALKER, Corporal, Michael.   Bay 6 and 7.

Arras Road Cemetery, Roclincourt

CHATWIN, Rifleman, Leonard Henry.   Grave Ref. II. N. 37.

Athies Communal Cemetery Extension
BUTLER, Private, Harry.   Grave Ref. H. 13.
Auchonvillers Military Cemetery
ALLTON, Private, William.   Grave Ref II. B.18
Aveluy Communal Cemetery Extension, Somme
MIDDLETON, Gunner, Alfred George. Grave Ref. G. 45.
Awoingt British Cemetery, Nord
MEYRICK, Private, James Ivor.   Grave Ref. III. B. 7.
Bienvillers Military Cemetery
COPE, Sergeant , Walter.   Grave Ref. I. A. 65.
MALLABONE, Lnce Cpl, Thomas.   Grave Ref. III. A. 4.
Boulogne Eastern Cemetery, Pas de Calais
HASTINGS, Private, William George.   Grave Ref. VIII. D. 199.
WALKER, Private, John Thomas.   Grave Ref. VIII. I. 6.
Browns Copse Cemetery, Roeux
SPARROW, Private, Frederick. Grave Ref. II. D. 26.
Busigny Communal Cemetery Extension
BRINDLEY, Private, George.   Grave Ref. III. B. 7.
FARNDON, Private, Albert   Grave Ref. III. B. 8.
Cambrin Military Cemetery
JEE, Sapper, Harry.   Grave Ref. B. 11
Choques Military Cemetery
LEACH, Private, Bert.   Grave Ref I. G. 79.
SAUNDERS, Private, Edmund.   Grave Ref. IV. D. 35.
Corbie Communal Cemetery Extension
MOORE, Private, William Alfred.   Grave Ref. 2. E. 36.
Croisilles British Cemetery, Pas de Calais
TALLIS, Private, Joseph.   Grave Ref. I. B. 16.
Cross Roads Cemetery, Fontaine-Au-Bois, Nord
KNIGHT, Private, Albert John.   Grave Ref. III. A. 10.
Crump Trench British Cemetery, Fampoux.
SMITH, Lance Corporal, Walter.   Grave Ref. II. B. 25.
Daours Communal Cemetery Extension
TUDGE, Private, Walter George Albert. Grave Ref. VI. A. 15.

Delville Wood Cemetery, Longueval, Somme
CATER, Private, Edgar Percival.   Grave Ref. X. G. 6.
Etaples Military Cemetery, Pas de Calais
BRAY, Private, William H.   Grave Ref.XXXIII. E. 31A
GILBERT, Private, Joseph Gatcliff.   Grave Ref. XVIII. M. 8A.
Etretat Churchyard
JACQUES, Acting Corporal, William.   Grave Ref. II. C. 8.
Euston Road Cemetery, Colincamps
RANDLE, Private, Joseph.   Grave Ref. I. A. 33. *Feuchy*
British Cemetery
REYNOLDS, Private, Charles.   Grave Ref. I. C. 23.
Fifteen Ravine British Cemetery, Villiers Plouich
BURKS, Private, Henry.   Grave Ref. II. D. 12.
Flatiron Copse Cemetery, Mametz, Somme
WORTHINGTON, Gunner, William.   Grave Ref. X. J. 4.
Godewaersvelde British Cemetery, Nord
DAVIS, Private, Walter.   Grave Ref. I. J. 32.
STEVENS, Private, John Alfred.   Grave Ref. I. N. 34.
Grevillers British Cemetery
KNIGHT, Private, Albert.   Grave Ref. XII. D. 1.
Grove Town Cemetery, Meaulte
PICKER, Private, Frederick.   Grave Ref. II. E. 9.
Guards' Cemetery, Lesboeufs, Somme
RICHARDS, Guardsman,   Grave Ref. VII. F. 6.
Hargicourt British Cemetery, Aisne
VEARS, Private, Frederick William.   Grave Ref. I. F. 10.
Heilly Station Cemetery, Mericourt-L'abbe, Somme
GRIFFITH, Private, Arthur.   Grave Ref. IV. A. 6.
Hinges Military Cemetery
COTTON, Private, Fred Charles.   Grave Ref. C. 20.
Humbercamps Communal Cemetery Extension
ROWLAND, Private, Samuel.   Grave Ref. I. D. 7.
Laventie Military Cemetery, La Gorgue, Nord
ALLEN, Corporal, William John.   Grave Ref. II. C. 8
La Gorgue Communal Cemetery, Nord
TWIGGER, Acting Sergeant, Tom.   Grave Ref. IV. A. 3.

Le Touret Memorial

FRISWELL, Private, John Padbury.   Panel 26.

ISON, Private, Charles Albert.   Panel 2 and 3.

LEACH, Private, Isaac.   Panel 33 and 34.

RALLEY, Private, Abram.   Panel 6.

RANDLE, Private, Levi. Ref.   Panel 11.

SMALLEY, Private, Thomas.   Panel 15 and 16.

Longuenesse (St. Omer) Souvenir Cemetery, Pas de Calais

ALLEN, Corporal, William John.   Grave Ref. II. C. 8.

BRAY, Private, Norris William. T.   Grave Ref. IV. E. 82.

MORSON, Walter.   Grave Ref. IV. A. 31

Loos British Cemetery, France.

BROWN, Private, William.   Grave Ref. XX. E.

Loos Memorial, Pas de Calais

BATES, Private, Harold.   Panel 22 to 25

HAYWOOD, Private, Jesse.   Panel 22 to 25.

HOBBS, Private, Frank Alfred.   Panel 22 to 25.

HUNT, Lance Corporal, Stanley Albert. Panel 22 to 25.

NEALE, Private, Alexander Grant.   Panel 22 to 25.

TALLIS, Private, Thomas.   Panel 22 to 25.

TOPP, Private, Aubrey   Panel 22 to 25

WALKER, Private, Thomas William.   Addenda Panel.

WHITCROFT, Private, Tom.   Panel 22 to 25.

WILLS, Rifleman, Samuel Henry.   Panel 130 to 135.

Mendinghem Military Cemetery

BROWN, Corporal, Thomas.   Grave Ref. X. A. 24.

Meteren Military Cemetery

ROWLEY, Private, William H.   Grave Ref IV. C. 609.

Moeuvres Communal Cemetery Extension

NEALE, Private, Donald Grant.   Grave Ref. I. D. 2.

Mont Huon Military Cemetery, Le Treport, Seine-Maritime

FLETCHER, Lance Corporal, Isaac.   Grave Ref. VI. B. 1B.

Nesle Communal Cemetery

CANNON, Sergeant, Patrick.   Grave Ref. B. 1.

Outtersteene Communal Cemetery Extension, Bailleul,

BODELL, Lnce Cpl, George William.   Grave Ref. I. D. 32.

GILLAM, Private, Charles John.   Grave Ref. IV. A. 17.

Peronne Road Cemetery, Maricourt

RANDLE, Private, George. T.   Grave Ref. III. D. 7

Phalempin Communal Cemetery

GIBBERD, Private, Arthur Stanley.   Grave Ref. A. 1.

Point 110 New Military Cemetery, Fricourt, Somme

BAILEY, Private, John.   Grave Ref. E. 10.

FARNDON, Private, Herbert A.   Grave Ref. D. 12.

Pommereuil British Cemetery, Nord

PALMER, Private, Harry.   Grave Ref. D. 27

Pozieres Memorial, Somme

HARRISON, Lce Corporal, Thomas.   Panel 18 and 19

JACQUES, Private, Charles   Panel 54 to 56.

MARSTON, Lance Sergeant, Henry.   Panel 18 and 19.

ROWE, Pioneer, Charles Herbert.   Panel 10 to 13.

SMITH, Private, Oliver Thomas.   Panel 18 and 10.

Queant Road Cemetery, Buissy, Pas de Calais

BROADBENT, Able Seaman, Able.   Grave Ref. VIII. F. 27.

Regina Trench Cemetery, Grandcourt, Somme

FREEMAN, Second Lieutenant, Tom.   Grave Ref. V. A. 19.

Rocquigny-Equancourt Road British Cemetery, Manancourt

LAKIN, Private, Joseph John.   Grave Ref. XIV. A. 12.

Royal Irish Rifles Graveyard, Laventie

TIBBITTS, Private, Jack Abraham.   Grave Ref. III. K. 17.

Serre Road Cemetery No.2, Somme

HARDIMAN, Gunner, Thomas George. Grave Ref. VIII. D. 14

MARTIN, Private, Alfred.   Grave Ref. XXXVIII. C. 14.

SPENCER, John. Arnold.   Grave Ref. XL. F. 11.

Soissons Memorial

WRIGHT, Private, Ernest William.

St. Amand British Cemetery

HARRIS, Lance Corporal, Robert Frank. Grave Ref. V. A. 14

St. Aubert British Cemetery

SMITH, Private, Walter Henry.

St. Hilaire Cemetery Extension, Frevent
JOHNSON, Private, Thomas.   Grave Ref. C. 4.

St. Pierre Cemetery, Amiens, Somme
PHILLIPS, Private, George Noel.   Grave Ref. VIII. F. 3.

St. Pol British Cemetery, St. Pol-Sur-Ternoise, Pas de Calais
DAFFERN, Private, Thomas. H.   Grave Ref. I. E. 4.

St. Sever Cemetery, Rouen, Seine-Maritime
SPACEY, Private, John William.   Grave Ref. B. 25. 4.

Suzanne Communal Cemetery Extension
FATHERS, Gnr, Frederick William.   Grave Ref. E. 24.

Targelle Ravine British Cemetery, Villers-Guislain
HARVEY, Private, John T.   Grave Ref. A. 13.

Thiepval Anglo-French Cemetery, Authuile
WILSON, Private, Roland.   Grave Ref. II. G. 2.

Thiepval Memorial
BAILEY, Private, Ernest John.   Pier and Face 7B.
BARLOW, Private, John.   Pier and Face 9A 9B and 10B.
BIDDLE, Private, Frank.   Pier and Face 9A 9B and 10B.
BOWERS, Private, George.   Pier and Face 9A 9B and 10B.
CRUTCHLOW, Pte, Herman.   Pier and Face 9 A 9 B and 10 B.
DEAN, A/ Bdr, George Henry, MM.   Pier and Face 1A and 8A.
EVERITT, Private, Harry.   Pier and Face 9 A 9 B and 10 B.
GAMMAGE, LCpl, Albert.   Pier and Face 9A 9B and 10B.
GIBBS, Private Alfred.   Pier and Face 2 C and 3 A.
GOODE, Pte, Charles Henry.   Pier and Face 10 A and 10 D.
GRIFFIN, Private, Arthur.   Pier and Face 5 A and 6 C.
HARRISON, Private, William.   Pier and Face 9 A 9 B and 10 B.
HENSON, Pte, George Thomas.   Pier and Face 4A.
HEWITT, Rfn, Arthur Edward.   Pier and Face 13 A and 13 B.
HILL, Private, John Thomas.   Pier and Face 9 A 9 B and 10 B.
HILL, Private, Rowland William.   Pier and Face 9 A 9 B and 10 B.
HOBBS, Lance Corporal, John Allen.   Pier and Face 9 A 9 B and 10 B.
KEMP, Private, George Thos.   Pier and Face 9A 9B and 10B.
KIMBERLEY, Private, Reuben.   Pier and Face 9A 9B and 10B.
KNIGHT, Private, John.   Pier and Face 5C and 12C.

MOORE, Private, Joseph.   Pier and Face 10 A and 10 D.
MOORE, Private, Thomas.   Pier and Face 9 A 9 B and 10 B.
MOORE, Private, William.   Pier and Face 10 C 10D and 11 A.
MUSSON, Private, Ernest.   Pier and Face 9 A 9 B and 10 B.
PAGE, Corporal, Cyril Morson, MM. Pier and Face 9 A 9 B and 10 B.
PEGG, Private, Thomas.   Pier and Face 9 A 9 B and 10 B.
PULLIN, Sapper, Frank.   Pier and Face 8A and 8 D.
SMITH, Private, Arthur.   Pier and Face 9A 9B and 10B.
SMITH, Private, John Norman.   Pier and Face 8 C 9 A and 16 A.
SMITH, Private, William.   Pier and Face 9 A 9 B and 10 B.
SPENCER, Private, John Thomas.   Pier and Face 5 A and 6 C.
THORPE, Private, Richard.   Pier and Face 9A 9B and 10B.
TIDMAN, Private, Thomas.   Pier and Face 10 A and 10 D.
TYLER, Private, Peter.   Pier and Face 9 A 9 B and 10 B.
WILKINS, Pte, George Samuel. Pier and Face 9A 9B and 10B.
Verchain British Cemetery, Verchain-Maugre
JACQUES, Private, Amos William.   Grave Ref. A. 4.
Vieille-Chapelle New Military Cemetery, Lacouture
PAYNE, Private, Ernest.   Grave Ref. I. D. 5
PRIEST, Lance Corporal, William Joseph, MM. Grave Ref. I. D. 4.
Villiers-Bretonneux Memorial
LENTON, Private, Charles Joseph.
Villiers Plouich Communal Cemetery.
BURGESS, Private, William George.   Grave Ref. A. 26.
Vis-en-Artois Memorial
SMITH, Private, Walter.   Panel 3.

Germany
Worms (Hochheim Hill) Cemetery, Worms, Rheinland-Pfalz
SMITH, Private, William Ernest.   Screen Wall.

Greece
Doiran Memorial
BUCKNALL, Private, Thomas.
FULLYLOVE, Private, John.
SKINNER, Private, William Matthew.

Karasouli Military Cemetery
BIRD, Lance Corporal, James.   Grave Ref. F. 1349.
Pieta Military Cemetery
JACQUES, Private, Thomas.   Grave Ref.A.XXVIII. I.

India
Kirkee 1914-1918 Memorial,
GRIFFIN, Private, Walter. Face B.

Iraq
Amara War Cemetery
ARNOLD, Private, Charles. Sidney.   Grave Ref. XXIX. B. 41/51.
CRUTCHLOW, Private, Arthur.   Grave Ref. XXIV. C. 31.
DAVENPORT, Private, Sam.   Grave Ref. XXIV. F. 4.
FORD, Private, Edward, A.   Grave Ref. XIX. J. 10.
Basra Memorial and War Cemetery
AUSTIN, Corporal, Lawrence.   Grave Ref. VI. W. 1
AYRES, Lance Corporal, George William.   Panel 9.
CARTER, Private, Walter Harry.   Panel 9.
HAMMERSLEY, Private, Arthur.   Panel 34.
LONG, Private, Joseph.   Panel 9.
MARTIN, Private, Benjamin.   Panel 26 and 63.
TALLIS, Lance Corporal, William.   Panel 24.

Iran.
Tehran Memorial
REYNOLDS, Private, James.   Panel 2. Column 2.

Italy
Boscon British Cemetery
DERICOTT, Private, Thomas.   Grave Ref. 2. B. 13.
Cavalleto British Cemetery
EDWARDS, John Thomas   Grave Ref. I. F. 16.
Giavera Memorial
JOHNSON, Private, John.

Granezza British Cemetery
DARLISON, Private, Thomas.　　　　Grave Ref. 1. B. 9.

Turkey
Beach Cemetery, Anzac
TWIGGER, Private, Ernest.　　　　Grave Ref. II. E. 7.
Helles Memorial
EDWARDS Private, John.　　　　Panel 104 to 113
FOX, Sapper, Frederick Beauclerc.　　Panel 23,25
LOVETT, Private, Leonard.　　　　Panel 104 to 113.
SHARPE, Private, Israel.　　　　Panel 185 to 190.
SPEDING, Private, Tom.　　　　Panel 136 to 139.

United Kingdom
Bedworth Cemetery
BERRILL, Sapper, George. W.　　　Grave Ref. L. M. 37.
BOWNS, Private, Thomas Henry.　　Grave Ref. L. N. 42.
CONWAY, Private, George.　　　　Grave Ref. G. P. 19.
HARVEY, Walter.　　　　Grave Ref. I. L44.
MARPLES, Private, Henry.　　　　Grave Ref. B. N38.
PAGE, Private, Harry.　　　　Grave Ref. I. 122.
PARSONS, AM 3rd Cl, Ernest. R. F.　Grave Ref. L. K. 40.
PARSONS, Private, Victor Reginald.　Grave Ref. I. AA. 24.
TALLIS, Acting Corporal, William A.　Grave Ref. G. M. 4.
Coventry Cemetery
ROBINSON, Corporal, William.　　　Grave Ref. 197.143
Plymouth Naval Memorial, Devon.
CRUTCHLOW, Stoker, 1st Class, David. Panel 30
LUCAS, Able Seaman, Richard Bert.　Panel 7.
JONES, Able Seaman, Robert.　　　Panel 21.
Norton (All Saints) Churchyard.
PENN, Private, Harry.
Rothley Cemetery.
LOLE, Private, Harry.
Tottenham Cemetery, Middlesex.
BARTLETT, Bombardier, William.　　Grave Ref. Gen. 7337

Grave Locations: Bedworth Cemetery

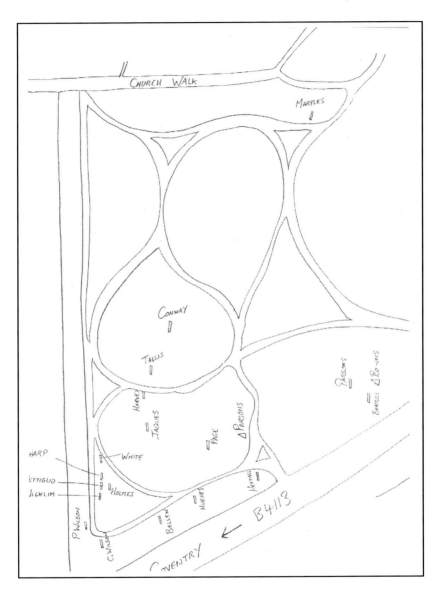

Those who served
Prisoners of War (Italics)

Abraham, J. W.	Royal Warwickshire Regiment
Adams, C.	Royal Warwickshire Regiment
Adams, F. L.	Royal Warwickshire Regiment
Adams, J.	Welsh Regiment
Adams, Richard.	Royal Warwickshire Regiment
Adams, Walter. E.	Royal Garrison Artillery
Adie, S.	Royal Warwickshire Regiment
Aldridge, A.	Machine Gun Corps
Aldridge, B.	Royal Field Artillery
Aldridge, F.	Royal Field Artillery
Aldridge, J.	Royal Field Artillery
Aldridge, J. T.	Royal Warwickshire Regiment
Aldridge, W.	Royal Warwickshire Regiment
Allen, A.	Royal Warwickshire Regiment
Allen, E. G.	Royal Warwickshire Regiment
Allen, F.	Royal W͏ ͏hire Regiment
Allen, Fred.	Machι ͏ps
Allen, F. H.	Hants
Allen, J. W.	R. M. A
Allton, A.	Royal G
Allton, Joseph W.	Grenadie
Archer, G.	Royal Arι
Armitage, E.	Royal War t
Armson, Walter.	Sherwood F
Arnold, Charles.	Royal Engine
Ashby, Frank.	Royal Warwiι
Ashby, Thomas	*Royal Warwicks*
Ashman, W.	Machine Gun C
Askill, J. W.	Gloucester Regin
Aubrey. A.	Royal Engineers
Aucott, D.	Worcestershire Regι
Ayres, J.	Royal Field Artillery
Bailey, A.	Royal Field Artillery

Bailey, T. W.	Coldstream Guards
Ball, F.	Coldstream Guards
Ball, J.	Coldstream Guards
Barfield, E.	Royal Warwickshire Regiment
Barlow, A.	Royal Berkshire Regiment
Barlow, W. A.	Royal Warwickshire Regiment
Barnett, A. R.	M. T., Royal Army Service Corps
Barnett, Edward.	Northants Regiment
Barnett, H.	Labour Corps
Barnett, Harold.	King's Liverpool Regiment
Barnett, S.	Oxfordshire and Buckinghamshire
Barnett, W.	Royal Warwickshire Regiment
Barraclough, C.	Oxfordshire and Buckinghamshire
Barraclough, F.	Worcestershire Regiment
Barrett, S.	Royal Field Artillery
Bass, J.	Royal Field Artillery
Bates, A.	HMS Sandringham
Bates, Samuel.	Royal Warwickshire Regiment
Bates, Thomas.	HMS Shannon
Beauman, J.	Royal Engineers
Beamish, J.	Tank Corps
Beamish, William.	Royal Marines
Beasley, A.	Royal Field Artillery
Beasley, Arthur.	Royal Engineers
Beasley, A. P.	A. V. C.
Beasley, George.	Wiltshire Regiment
Beasley, G. H.	Royal Warwickshire Regiment
Beasley, W.	Machine Gun Corps
Beddows, J.	Royal Berkshire Regiment
Beddows, J. MM	Gloucestershire Regiment
Beere, Harry.	Duke of Cornwall's Light Infantry
Beere, W.	Royal Warwickshire Regiment
Bennett, George. DCM. MM.	Royal Field Artillery
Bennett, T.	Gloucestershire Regiment
Bennett, W.	Royal Warwickshire Regiment
Bennett, W.	Somerset Light Infantry
Berrill, G. W.	Royal Engineers.

Berrill, S.	Gloucestershire Regiment
Bestwick, W. Harvey.	Army Ordnance Corps
Bicknell, F.	Royal Berkshire Regiment
Biddle, N.	Royal Warwickshire Regiment
Biddle, Sidney.	Duke of Cornwall's Light Infantry
Biddle, W.	Royal Warwickshire Regiment
Birch, F.	C. F. A.
Birch, J.	Royal Field Artillery
Birch, J. L.	Life Guards
Bird, G.	Royal Warwickshire Regiment
Bird, H. C.	Royal Engineers
Bird, J. L.	Life Guards
Bird, T. H.	Machine Gun Corps
Blake, F.	Royal Field Artillery
Blount, Edward.	Leicester Regiment
Blundred, J.	Devonshire Regiment
Blundred, J. T.	Royal Warwickshire Regiment
Blundred, Thomas H.	Royal Warwickshire Regiment
Blundred, W. H.	Royal Warwickshire Regiment
Bolden, W.	Royal Field Artillery
Bolstridge, A. J.	R. M. A.
Bolstridge, A. J.	Devonshire Regiment
Bolstridge, F. T.	R. M.E
Bolstridge, J.	Royal Warwickshire Regiment
Bolstridge, T. F.	HMS Arun
Bond, E. C.	Royal Army Service Corps
Bond, Isaac.	Somerset Light Infantry
Bone, A. H.	Royal Warwickshire Regiment
Bonser, J.	Royal Artillery
Bonsor, Bert.	Royal Engineers
Bonsor, J. K.	Royal Warwickshire Regiment
Booth, Harold V.	Devonshire Regiment
Bosworth, B.	Dorsetshire Regiment
Bosworth, D. A.	M. T., RASC
Bosworth, Fred A. MM	Royal Field Artillery
Bosworth, H. K.	Royal Army Medical Corps
Botterill, G.	Machine Gun Corps

Boycott, E.	Gloucestershire Regiment
Bradbury, C. G. W.	Tank Corps
Bradbury, Chas. Sidney	Royal Field Artillery
Bradshaw, W.	*Oxfordshire and Buckinghamshire*
Brandist, E.	Royal Warwickshire Regiment
Brandist, J.	Royal Marines
Brandist, John.	Royal Warwickshire Regiment
Bradshaw, J.	Duke of Cornwall's Light Infantry
Bray, Thomas.	Royal Navy
Brindley, J.	Wiltshire Regiment
Brindley, J.	Royal Garrison Artillery
Brindley, T.	Royal Warwickshire Regiment
Brindley, W. N.	Machine Gun Corps
Broadbent, J.	Royal Warwickshire Regiment
Broadway, G. Thomas.	Royal Warwickshire Regiment
Brookes, J.	HMS Caroline
Brookes, R. A.	Royal Warwickshire Regiment
Brown, B. H.	Royal Air Force
Brown, Ernest.	Royal W. Fusiliers
Brown, F.	King's Royal Rifle Corps
Brown, John.	Royal Warwickshire Regiment
Brown, Sam.	Grenadier Guards
Brunsden, H. E.	Royal Garrison Artillery
Buckley, J.	Royal Warwickshire Regiment
Bucknall, E.	Royal Horse Artillery
Bucknall, George.	Royal Warwickshire Regiment
Bucknall, H.	Royal Warwickshire Regiment
Bucknall, Thomas. MM	Royal Garrison Artillery
Bucknall, Thomas. DCM	Royal Engineers
Bull, B. T.	Hants. Regiment
Bull, Chas. W.	Royal Warwickshire Regiment
Bull, Thos. A.	Royal Warwickshire Regiment
Bunney, Aubrey F.	HMS Diligence
Burbury, H.	Royal Warwickshire Regiment
Burbury, J.	Royal Warwickshire Regiment
Burbury, W.	Royal Warwickshire Regiment
Burgess, E.	Royal Berkshire Regiment

Burgess, Harry.	Royal Engineers
Burgess, T. H.	Royal Marine Light Infantry
Burgess, W. G.	Royal Berkshire Regiment
Burton, Ernest.	Coldstream Guards
Butler, A.	Dorsets Regiment
Butler, Harry.	Oxfordshire and Buckinghamshire
Butler, J.	Royal Field Artillery
Butler, Sidney.	Royal Berkshire Regiment
Butler, Thos.	Oxfordshire and Buckinghamshire
Campion	King's Own Yorkshire Light Infantry
Cannon, J.	Royal Engineers
Carding, T. H.	Royal Warwickshire Regiment
Carding, W. H. MC	South African
Carding, W. V.	Coldstream Guards
Carey, T.	Royal Warwickshire Regiment
Carter, Amos. G.	Royal Warwickshire Regiment
Carter, Chas.	Royal Field Artillery
Carter, George.	Royal Warwickshire Regiment
Carter, Sam.	Royal Warwickshire Regiment
Carvell, W. MM	Oxfordshire and Buckinghamshire
Case, A. E.	HMS Michael
Case, J.	Grenadier Guards
Cashmore, G.	Royal Field Artillery
Cashmore, R. J.	Devons Regiment
Cater, J. S.	P. P. C. L.I.
Cater, L.	West Yorkshire Regiment
Cave, T.	Royal Garrison Artillery
Chamberlain, A.	Cheshire Regiment
Chapman, F.	Machine Gun Corps
Chatwin, E.	M. F. P.
Chatwin, E. F.	Royal Warwickshire Regiment
Chatwin, J.	Dorsets Regiment
Childs, Charles.	Royal Warwickshire Regiment
Claridge, G. W.	Royal Warwickshire Regiment
Clarke, Enoch.	Royal Warwickshire Regiment
Clarke, G. B.	Royal Field Artillery
Clarke, I. G.	Australian A. S. C.

Clarke, Isaac.	Cyclist Corps.
Clarke, J.	Royal Warwickshire Regiment
Clarke, Josiah.	Coldstream Guards
Clarke, Richard.	Royal Warwickshire Regiment
Clarke, W. E.	Trench Mortar Battery
Claydon, A.	Royal Warwickshire Regiment
Clayton, G. W.	O. C. B.
Cleaver, J.	West Yorkshire Regiment
Cleaver, L. J.	Machine Gun Corps
Clifford, Frank.	Labour Corps
Clifford, George.	Royal Field Artillery
Clones, Harry.	Labour Corps
Cluley, A. MM	London Regiment
Cockerill, John.	19th Lancers
Cole, A.	Royal Warwickshire Regiment
Cole, C.	Machine Gun Corps
Coleman, Arthur.	Royal Warwickshire Regiment
Coley, Joseph.	Royal Field Artillery
Collins, G.	Royal Berkshire Regiment
Colgan, A. G.	Royal Engineers
Cooke, A. D.	London Regiment
Cooke, J.	Royal Engineers
Cooke, Jesse.	Oxfordshire and Buckinghamshire
Cooke, Sid.	Royal Artillery
Coombe, P. H.	War. Yeo. Machine Gun Corps
Coombes, Harry.	Hampshire Regiment.
Cooper, A.	Royal Flying Corps
Cooper, G.	Machine Gun Corps
Cooper, G.	Royal Warwickshire Regiment
Cooper, H. S.	Guards M. G. Regiment
Cooper, J. H.	Royal Warwickshire Regiment
Cooper, J. R.	Devons Regiment
Cooper, J. R.	South Staffordshire Regiment
Copeland, J.	Royal Artillery
Copeland, Jesse.	Oxfordshire and Buckinghamshire
Copeland, R.	Royal Warwickshire Regiment
Cornish, J. T.	Royal Field Artillery

Cornish, W. C.	Manchester Regiment
Cosgrave, F. R.	Dorset Regiment
Cotton, Samuel.	Royal Warwickshire Regiment
Coughton, J.	Oxfordshire and Buckinghamshire
Courts, A. E.	Royal Fusiliers
Courts, A. J.	Royal Warwickshire Regiment
Cramp, James.	Royal Warwickshire Regiment
Creswell, G.	Royal Field Artillery
Crisp, O. G.	Durham Light Infantry
Crisp, O. J.	Royal Engineers.
Croft, Arthur.	Machine Gun Corps
Croft, Arthur	Hampshire Regiment
Croft, F. T.	Royal Field Artillery
Croxall, A. MM	Oxfordshire and Buckinghamshire
Crutchlow, A.	Somerset Light Infantry
Crutchlow, Arthur	Royal Warwickshire Regiment
Crutchlow, C. W.	Royal Warwickshire Regiment
Crutchlow, D.	HMS Narborough
Crutchlow, Ernest.	Royal Engineers
Crutchlow, Joseph.	Royal Warwickshire Regiment
Cunningham, John.	East Lancashire Regiment
Curtis, Jack.	North Staffordshire Regiment
Daffern, C. J.	*South Staffordshire Regiment*
Daffern, Frederick Sydney	Australian Infantry
Daffern, H. W.	Royal Scots
Daffern, John.	Devons Regiment
Daffern, J.	London Rangers
Daffern, N.	Trench Mortars
Daffern, William.	King's Liverpool Regiment
Daffern, W. MM	Royal Field Artillery
Daft, Fred.	Royal Warwickshire Regiment
Dale, John.	Royal Warwickshire Regiment
Daley, R.	Lancashire Fusiliers
Dalton, J.	Leicestershire Regiment
Dalton, Thomas.	Royal Engineers
Darby, William.	Royal Army Medical Corps
Darker, Wm.	Can. For. Corps

Darlaston, A. J.	*Oxfordshire and Buckinghamshire*
Darlaston, S.	Oxfordshire and Buckinghamshire
Darlaston, S.	Coldstream Guards
Darlaston, W.	Grenadier Guards
Darlison	Grenadier Guards
Darlison, E.	Royal Field Artillery
Darlison, H.	Royal Air Force
Darlison, J. H.	Royal Army Medical Corps
Darlison, T.	Royal Field Artillery
Davenport, Walter.	Machine Gun Corps
Davies, A.	R. S. C.
Davies, A. Victor.	Royal Warwickshire Regiment
Davies, G.	Royal Army Service Corps
Davies, Job.	Royal Garrison Artillery
Davies, W. D.	Royal Artillery
Davis, J.	Army Service Corps
Day, E. A.	Royal Air Force
Deeming, Fred.	Mob. Vet. S. R. A. S. C.
Deeming, H.	London Regiment
Deeming, John.	Oxfordshire and Buckinghamshire
Dewis, Ben.	Royal Warwickshire Regiment
Dewis, Charles.	Oxfordshire and Buckinghamshire
Dewis, D.	Royal Field Artillery
Dewis, E.	Gloucestershire Regiment
Dewis, Fred.	Royal Engineers
Dewis, Fred.	Worcestershire Regiment
Dewis, George.	Royal Field Artillery
Dewis, Harry.	Grenadier Guards
Dewis, John.	London Scottish
Dewis, Joseph.	Grenadier Guards
Dewis, Joseph.	Royal Air Force
Dewis, Thomas.	HMS Minotaur
Dickens, James E.	Gloucestershire Regiment
Dickens, Joseph.	Gloucestershire Regiment
Dix, J.	Royal Field Artillery
Docker, E. E.	Oxfordshire and Buckinghamshire
Dodd, E.	Royal Warwickshire Regiment

Dodsworth, J. W.	Royal Air Force
Downing, W. E.	Royal Garrison Artillery
Downs, J.	Tank Corps
Drakeford, A.	Royal Warwickshire Regiment
Drakeford, T. R.	T. R. Batt.
Drakeford, W. H.	Gloucestershire Regiment
Drayford, J. T.	Royal Warwickshire Regiment
Dunkley, J. B. C. de G.	Royal Engineers
Dyall, George.	Royal Warwickshire Regiment
Dyall, John T.	Machine Gun Corps
Dyke, E.	Royal Warwickshire Regiment
Eabry, N. C.	O. C. B.
Earl, L. E.	Royal Berkshire Regiment
Earp, W. H.	Royal Warwickshire Regiment
Eaton, J.	Royal Warwickshire Regiment
Edmands, E.	Royal Marine Light Infantry
Edmands, F. Scott.	Middlesex Yeomanry
Edmands, J.	Royal Army Medical Corps
Edmands, J.	Grenadier Guards
Edwards, W. J.	Royal Fusiliers
Elliott, A.	Lincolnshire Regiment
Elliott, A. H.	Royal Warwickshire Regiment
Elliott, F. J.	R. E. R. M. R
Elliott, J. W.	Leicestershire Regiment
Evans, A.	Royal Field Artillery
Everitt, F.	Royal Warwickshire Regiment
Everitt, J. T.	Somerset Light Infantry
Every, J. T.	Royal Warwickshire Regiment
Fairbrother, Frederick.	Borderers
Falcon, W.	Royal Fusiliers
Fallis	Oxfordshire and Buckinghamshire
Farley, C. R.	Royal Warwickshire Regiment
Farley, J. W.	Worcestershire Regiment
Farley, T. P.	Duke of Cornwalls Light Infantry
Farmer, A.	Royal Warwickshire Regiment
Fardon, Arthur.	Royal Warwickshire Regiment
Farndon, A. E.	Grenadier Guards

Farndon, E. J.	Royal Warwickshire Regiment
Farndon, E. W.	Royal Warwickshire Regiment
Farndon, Frank.	Royal Engineers
Farndon, Jesse.	Royal Welsh Fusiliers
Farndon, Joseph. MM	Royal Field Artillery
Farndon, Sidney.	Royal Warwickshire Regiment
Farndon, W. G.	Worcestershire Regiment
Farndon, W. H.	Royal Warwickshire Regiment
Felton, John.	Royal Field Artillery
Felton, Samuel.	Royal Navy
Felton, Thomas.	Royal Field Artillery
Felton, William Jun.	Royal Field Artillery
Felton, William Sen.	Royal Warwickshire Regiment
Finch, T.	Royal Engineers
Flale, J.	Royal Field Artillery
Flanaghan, E. E.	North Staffordshire Regiment
Flanaghan, E. G.	Coldstream Guards
Flanaghan, George.	Royal Engineers
Flanaghan, T.	King's Liverpool Regiment
Flanaghan, Tom.	Devons Regiment
Flavell, H.	Dorset Works Bn
Flavell, Geo.	Leicestershire Regiment
Fletcher, H. E.	Coldstream Guards
Fletcher, Jack.	Royal Warwickshire Regiment
Foley, S.	Royal Warwickshire Regiment
Ford, A.	Oxfordshire and Buckinghamshire
Ford, Alf. J.	King's Royal Rifles
Ford. A. S.	Royal Warwickshire Regiment
Ford, Edward A.	Royal Field Artillery
Ford, I. J.	Wiltshire Regiment
Ford, Stanley.	South Staffordshire Regiment
Ford, Thomas.	Oxfordshire and Buckinghamshire
Ford, W. C.	Royal Garrison Artillery
Ford, W. H.	Royal Warwickshire Regiment
Forster, A.	Royal Field Artillery
Forster, I. E.	Devons Regiment
Foster, William.	Rifle Brigade

Fradgley, Chas.	Royal Engineers
Freeman, Harry.	HMS Revenge
Freeman, Sam.	Royal Warwickshire Regiment
French, W.	Oxfordshire and Buckinghamshire
Friswell, Chas.	Royal Warwickshire Regiment
Friswell, Joseph.	Labour Corps
Froggett, G.	Machine Gun Corps
Froggett, H.	Devons Regiment
Froggett, James.	Royal Engineers
Froggett, R.	M. T., R. A. S. C.
Fullylove, A.	Royal Warwickshire Regiment
Galland, J.	Royal Warwickshire Regiment
Gallemore, F.	Somerset Light Infantry
Garner, C.	Royal Field Artillery
Garner, G.	Royal Field Artillery
Garrett, Richard.	Oxfordshire and Buckinghamshire
Gazey, J.	Royal Engineers
Gazey, J.	Royal Warwickshire Regiment
Gazey, Robert S.	Sherwood Foreseters
Gee, John.	Royal Berkshire Regiment.
Gee, J. H.	Oxfordshire and Buckinghamshire
Gee John F.	*Royal Warwickshire Regiment*
Gee, J. H.	*Royal Warwickshire Regiment*
Gee, Walter.	HMS Princess Royal
Gibberd, Alfred.	South African Force
Gibberd, Erakine. MM	Royal Field Artillery
Gibberd, Eustace.	Canadian Expeditionary Force
Gibbs, G. W.	Royal Warwickshire Regiment
Gilbert, F.	Machine Gun Corps
Gilbert (Bom'r)	Royal Field Artillery
Gilbert, F.	Royal Field Artillery
Gilbert, John.	HMS Leopard
Gilbert, Oliver.	Royal Field Artillery
Gilbert, Thomas.	Royal Field Artillery
Gilbert, W. H.	Royal Engineers
Gilbey, A.	Royal Warwickshire Regiment
Gillert	Royal Field Artillery

Glover, B.	Royal Warwickshire Regiment
Glover, W. C.	Royal Warwickshire Regiment
Golby, A.	Dorsets Regiment
Golby, A.	Devons Regiment
Golby, J. E.	Royal Engineers
Golby. J. H.	North Devon Hussars
Golby, J. H.	Royal Warwickshire Regiment
Golby, J.	Oxfordshire and Buckinghamshire
Golby, J.	Cambridgeshire Regiment
Golby, William.	Royal Field Artillery
Golby, W. H.	Royal Engineers
Golder, Caleb.	Oxfordshire and Buckinghamshire
Gomm, G.	Royal Engineers
Goode, Andrew.	Royal Warwickshire Regiment
Goode, B. W.	Machine Gun Corps
Goode, T. H.	Middlesex Yeomanry
Goodyer, J. W.	Oxfordshire and Buckinghamshire
Goodyer, S.	Cornwall Pioneer Battalion
Gosling, E.	Royal Warwickshire Regiment
Green, C. A.	Rifle Brigade
Green, George.	Royal Field Artillery
Green, R.	King's African Rifles
Greenway, W. H.	Grenadier Guards
Greenhough, Frank.	Oxfordshire and Buckinghamshire
Gregory, Herbert.	King's Dragoon Guards
Gregory, H.	*Royal Marine Light Infantry*
Griffin, Arthur.	Worcestershire Regiment
Griffin, G.	Royal Engineers
Griffin, G.	East Yorkshire Pioneers
Griffin, J.	Royal Welsh Fusiliers
Griffin, Thomas.	Royal Warwickshire Regiment
Griffiths, A.	Oxfordshire and Buckinghamshire
Griffiths, J.	HMS Tamar
Grimley, I. S.	Royal Engineers
Gudger	Oxfordshire and Buckinghamshire
Gurney, A.	Royal Warwickshire Regiment
Haddon, C. E.	Royal Warwickshire Regiment

Haddon, John Thos.	Royal Air Force
Haddon, W.	Royal Field Artillery
Hadley, G.	Royal Engineers
Hale, J.	Royal Field Artillery
Hall, G. F.	Royal Army Medical Corps
Hall, J. H.	Dragoon Guards
Hall, S.	Durham Light Infantry
Hall, T. E.	Royal Engineers
Hall, Thos.	HMS Neptune
Hall, Wm.	Royal Warwickshire Regiment
Harris, H.	Royal Garrison Artillery
Harrison, Bert.	*Royal Warwickshire Regiment*
Hartlett, J. J.	Coldstream Guards
Hartlett, J.	Machine Gun Corps
Hartopp, Horace.	Royal Engineers
Hartopp, Harry, Sen.	Royal Engineers
Harvey, John.	Rifle Brigade
Harvey, J.	Royal Engineers
Harvey, J. L.	13th Hussars
Harvey, J. T.	Highland Light Infantry
Hastings, W.	Royal Warwickshire Regiment
Hawkins, H.	Royal Warwickshire Regiment
Hawkins, John.	Royal Engineers
Haynes, John.	Royal Warwickshire Regiment
Hay, Herbert.	West Riding Regiment
Haywood, Arthur.	Royal Air Force
Haywood, F.	Duke of Cornwall's Light Infantry
Haywood, J.	Gloucestershire Regiment
Haywood, John.	*Royal Warwickshire Regiment*
Haywood, O.	Devons Regiment
Haywood, Oliver.	Worcestershire Regiment
Haywood, Samuel.	Royal Warwickshire Regiment
Haywood, William.	Royal Warwickshire Regiment
Henson, Hubert.	Royal Field Artillery
Henson, G.	Labour Corps
Henton, Joseph.	HMS Ladar
Henton, Sam.	Hawke Battalion

Henton, S.	Royal Warwickshire Regiment
Herbert, A. W.	Royal Warwickshire Regiment
Herbert, W.	Royal Warwickshire Regiment
Hewitt, Jonathon.	Royal Army Service Corps
Hewitt, P.	Royal Flying Corps
Hewitt, T.	Royal Garrison Artillery
Hextall, A.	Royal Army Service Corps
Hextall, Frank.	Royal Berkshire Regiment
Hill, A. J.	Royal Army Medical Corps
Hill, H.	Royal Warwickshire Regiment
Hill, John.	Royal Field Artillery
Hillyard, F.	Royal Army Service Corps
Hirons, J.	Sherwood Foresters
Hirons, William T.	Royal Defence Corps
Hobbs, A.	Royal Warwickshire Regiment
Hobbs, Oswald.	Royal Engineers
Hobday, W. H.	Worcestershire Regiment
Hobday	Machine Gun Corps
Hogben, J.	King's Royal Rifles
Holding, W.	Royal Warwickshire Regiment
Holland, James.	Royal Warwickshire Regiment
Homer, Ed Hy.	HMS Greenwich
Honour, T. A.	Royal Field Artillery
Hood, A.	Royal Warwickshire Regiment
Hood, Alf.	Oxfordshire and Buckinghamshire
Hood, Harry.	Grenadier Guards
Hood, Joe.	Northants Regiment
Hood, W. H.	Royal Garrison Artillery
Hopewell, Arthur.	*Royal Warwickshire Regiment*
Hopkins, A. T.	Devons Regiment
Hopkins, B.	Gloucestershire Regiment
Hopkins, W. J.	Royal Warwickshire Regiment
Horne, A.	Machine Gun Corps
Horton, Fred.	Royal Engineers
Horton, H.	Coldstream Guards
Horton, T.	Royal Warwickshire Regiment
Hough, George.	Tank Corps

181

Howe, Bert. MM	Royal Field Artillery
Howe, J. W.	M.T., Royal Army Service Corps
Howe, H. MM	Royal Army Service Corps
Hughes, L.	Oxfordshire and Buckinghamshire
Hughes, W.	Royal Garrison Artillery
Hunt, A. E.	*Royal Warwickshire Regiment*
Hunt, P. W.	Machine Gun Corps
Hunt, P. W.	Duke of Cornwall's Light Infantry
Hurst, C. C. W.	Coldstream Guards
Hurst, R. G.	A. P. C.
Hutt, Ben.	Royal Warwickshire Regiment
Ison, Arthur.	Machine Gun Corps
Ison, James.	*Worcestershire Regiment*
Jackson, Alfred.	Labour Corps
Jackson, Edward.	Royal Warwickshire Regiment
Jackson, F. G.	*Royal Warwickshire Regiment*
Jackson, H.	Somerset Light Infantry
Jackson, John.	Dorsets Regiment
Jackson, Walter.	HMS Seagull
Jackson, Wm.	Gloucestershire Regiment
Jackson, W.	Royal Warwickshire Regiment
Jacques, Ben.	*Royal Naval Division*
Jacques, H.	Royal Warwickshire Regiment
Jacques, I. H.	Royal Garrison Artillery
Jacques, Joseph.	Royal Engineers
Jacques, Joseph.	Royal Warwickshire Regiment
Jacques, S.	Royal Engineers
Jacques, S.	Royal Warwickshire Regiment
Jacques, S.	Coldstream Guards
Jacques, T.	Tank Corps
James, H. W.	Royal Army Medical Corps
Jaques, Fred.	Highland Light Infantry
Jee, George.	Royal Engineers
Jee, Joseph.	Oxfordshire and Buckinghamshire
Jee, Wm.	Gloucestershire Regiment
Jeffs, W. T.	Royal Field Artillery
Johnson, Frank.	Royal Warwickshire Regiment

Johnson, G.	Royal Dragoons
Johnson, G. H.	Royal Warwickshire Regiment
Johnson, G. W.	Royal Warwickshire Regiment
Johnson, J.	Sherwood Foresters
Johnson, Jim.	Royal Fusiliers
Johnson, John D.	Warwickshire Yeomanry
Johnson, W.	Royal Warwickshire Regiment
Jones, A.	Royal Field Artillery
Jones, E. T.	Tank Corps
Jones, George.	Labour Corps
Jones, George.	Worcestershire Regiment
Jones, Henry.	Royal Warwickshire Regiment
Jones, Horace.	Machine Gun Corps
Jones, John T.	Royal Engineers
Juby, O.	Royal Warwickshire Regiment
Judd, E. T.	Royal Fusiliers
Kelley, H.	Worcestershire Regiment
Kelsey, Ernest J.	Royal Fusiliers
Kelsey, W	Machine Gun Corps
Kemp, A. G.	Gloucestershire Regiment
Kennedy, Peter	Royal Marine Light Infantry
Kenney, A	London Regiment
Kidger, J.	Tank Corps
Kidger, Herbert	Worcestershire Regiment
Kimberley, E.	Royal Warwickshire Regiment
Kinder, J. H.	Gloucestershire Regiment
Kinder, J. T.	Royal Warwickshire Regiment
King, A. B.	Royal Warwickshire Regiment
Knibbs, Jas.	Oxfordshire and Buckinghamshire
Knight, Alfred	Royal Warwickshire Regiment
Knight, Ernest	Royal Field Artillery
Knight, F.	Royal Warwickshire Regiment
Knight, T.	Royal Warwickshire Regiment
Knight, Wm. T.	Royal Warwickshire Regiment
Lakin, C.	Oxfordshire and Buckinghamshire
Lakin, I. L.	T. R. O.
Lakin, Fred	Royal Warwickshire Regiment

Lakin, F.	Royal Warwickshire Regiment
Lathbury, H. W.	Royal Warwickshire Regiment
Lawrence, A. H.	Royal Warwickshire Regiment
Leach, Ernest	Royal Warwickshire Regiment
Leach, John. MM	Royal Warwickshire Regiment
Leach, W. H.	Royal Field Artillery
Lee, A. E. R.	M. M. G. C.
Lee, David	Royal Garrison Artillery
Lee, E. T.	Dorsets Regiment
Lee, Henry	Royal Army Service Corps
Lee, Henry	Durham Light Infantry
Lee, L.	Grenadier Guards
Lee, L. G.	Somerset Light Infantry
Lee, Leslie	
Lee, Samuel	M. T., R.A. S. C.
Lee, W.	Royal Engineers
Lee, W. H.	*Somerset Light Infantry*
Lee, W. O.	Oxfordshire and Buckinghamshire
Lenton, J.	Dorsets Regiment
Lenton, W. T.	Royal Field Artillery
Lenton, W. T.	Lancashire Fusiliers
Lenton, W.	T. R. B
Lewis, A. S.	Royal Warwickshire Regiment
Liggins, J.	Royal Field Artillery
Lloyd, T. H.	Royal Warwickshire Regiment
Lole, F. William.	Royal Field Artillery
Lole, Jack	Worcestershire Regiment
Lole, Percival. T.	Royal Field Artillery
Lovett, Roland	Royal Field Artillery
Lowe, J. H.	Royal Irish Rifles
Lownds, W.	Royal Engineers
Lucas, Cecil	Machine Gun Corps
Lucas, F. J. MM	Royal West Kent Regiment
Lucas, F. J.	Gloucestershire Regiment
Lucas, Harry	Somerset Light Infantry
Lucas, R.	Devons Regiment

Ludgate, G.	Oxfordshire and Buckinghamshire
Ludgate, H.	Oxfordshire and Buckinghamshire
Ludgate, L.	Oxfordshire and Buckinghamshire
Lydster, Thomas	Royal Warwickshire Regiment
Lyons, Harry	19th Hussars
Macey, R.	Royal Field Artillery
Macey, Thos.	Dragoon Guards
Magson, Alfred	Royal Engineers
Magson, Walter	Royal Field Artillery
Mainwaring	Royal Warwickshire Regiment
Mallabone, J. T.	Royal Engineers
Marlow, A. Ben.	Northants Regiment
Marlow, S.	Gloucestershire Regiment
Marriott, A.	Royal Warwickshire Regiment
Marriott, I.	Royal Field Artillery
Marsden, H. S.	*Norfolk Regiment*
Marsden, Reg.	Royal Field Artillery
Marsden, W.	Grenadier Guards
Marsh, F.	Royal Warwickshire Regiment
Marshall, E.	Royal Warwickshire Regiment
Marshall, Ernest L.	*Royal Warwickshire Regiment*
Marshall, J.	Royal Warwickshire Regiment
Marshall, R.	Royal Field Artillery
Marson, W. H.	Royal Warwickshire Regiment
Marston, B.	Royal Engineers
Marston, F.	Royal Warwickshire Regiment
Marston, Harrry	Royal Warwickshire Regiment
Marston, J.	Royal Field Artilly
Marston, J.	Royal Inniskilling Fusiliers
Marston, Sam	Royal Berkshire Regiment
Martin, Bert	Royal Warwickshire Regiment
Massey, D.	Royal Berkshire Regiment
Massey, Thomas.	*Royal Warwickshire Regiment*
McDonagh, A.	Coldstream Guards
Mercer, J. C.	R. N. D. H.
Meyrick, A.	Royal Warwickshire Regiment
Meyrick, E. A.	Machine Gun Corps

Meyrick, Edgar. MM	Royal Warwickshire Regiment
Meyrick, R.	Royal Field Artillery
Meyrick, W. H.	Royal Field Artillery
Miles, E. J.	Machine Gun Corps
Milliner, T.	Gloucestershire Regiment
Mills, E.	Royal Field Artillery
Mills, T.	Royal Army Service Corps
Mills, W. G.	Somerset Light Infantry
Mobbs, W. H.	Coldstream Guards
Mockford, E.	Royal Field Artillery
Mockford, J.	Royal Field Artillery
Moore, B. H.	*Royal Warwickshire Regiment*
Moore, E.	Royal Warwickshire Regiment
Moore, Ephraim	East Surrey Regiment
Moore, F.	Royal Garrison Artillery
Moore, H. H.	Machine Gun Battery
Moore, John	Royal Field Artillery
Moore, J. T.	Duke of Cornwall's Light Infantry
Moore, T.	Royal Warwickshire Regiment
Moore, Walter	Royal Warwickshire Regiment
Moore, W.	Queens R. W. S.
Moore, Wm.	Royal Warwickshire Regiment
Moore, W.	Machine Gun Corps
Moore, W.	Royal Warwickshire Regiment
Moore, Wm. J.	Royal Warwickshire Regiment
Morgan, G. H.	Royal Artillery
Morgan	Royal Army Service Corps
Morris, H. R.	Royal Warwickshire Regiment
Morris, S. W.	Royal Warwickshire Regiment
Morris, W. T.	Oxfordshire and Buckinghamshire
Morson, George	*Wiltshire Regiment*
Mosley, T. H.	Royal Army Service Corps
Moseley, H.	Royal Warwickshire Regiment
Mortiboy, B.	Scottish Rifles
Mountford, G. MM	Royal Field Artillery
Mountford, H.	Royal Warwickshire Regiment
Mountford, A. H.	Army Service Corps

Mountford, Harry R.	Royal Engineers
Neale, Arthur	Oxfordshire and Buckinghamshire
Neale, A. W.	Worcestershire Regiment
Neale, Ben.	Duke of Cornwall's Light Infantry
Neale, C. J.	Royal Engineers
Neale, J.	Royal Warwickshire Regiment
Neale, Jack	Royal Engineers
Neale, Joseph	Royal Warwickshire Regiment
Neale, Oliver	Royal Warwickshire Regiment
Neale, S. J.	Royal Engineers
Neale, Thos.	Royal Warwickshire Regiment
Neale, Thomas	262nd Inf. Brigade
Neale, W.	Royal Berkshire Regiment
Neale, William	Royal Warwickshire Regiment
Neale, Willliam	Worcestershire Regiment
Needham, J. A.	Royal Marine Light Infantry
Newitt, J.	Royal Air Force
Newman, Ar. Ern.	Leicestershire Regiment
Newman, John	Royal Warwickshire Regiment
Newman, H.	Worcestershire Regiment
Newman, H. E.	Royal Engineers
Newman, S	Royal Air Force
Niblett, F. A.	Royal Warwickshire Regiment
Niblett, R. G.	Dorsets Regiment
Nicholls, J.	Devons Regiment
Nicklin, Arthur	Royal Marine Light Infantry
Nicklin, A. H.	Devons Regiment
Nicklin, A. C.	Royal Engineers
Nicklin, J.	Labour Corps
Nicklin, J.	Oxfordshire and Buckinghamshire
Nicklin, S. J.	Royal Engineers
Nicklin, Tom C.	Oxfordshire and Buckinghamshire
Nicklin, W.	Royal Field Artillery
Nicklin, W. H.	Royal Marine Light Infantry
Nightingale, D.	Royal Field Artillery
Nightingale, J.	Royal Field Artillery
Nightingale, G.	Royal Field Artillery

187

Nightingale, R. E.	M. T. ,R. A. S. C.
Nightingale, R. E.	Devons Regiment
Nightingale, T.	Royal Field Artillery
Noon, T.	Machine Gun Corps
Nortney, J.	Royal Engineers
Odell, John	Royal Warwickshire Regiment
O'Grady, Peter	Royal Dublin Fusiliers
Oliver, E.	Royal Berkshire Regiment
Olorenshaw, W. T.	Royal Warwickshire Regiment
Orme, John	Royal Field Artillery
Orton, A.	Royal Warwickshire Regiment
Orton, C.	Royal Berkshire Regiment
Orton, F. A.	Norfolks Regiment
Orton, J.	Royal Berkshire Regiment
Orton, Joe	Royal Warwickshire Regiment
Orton, John. E.	Royal Army Medical Corps
Oulton, Thos. J.	Royal Warwickshire Regiment
Owen, Isaac F.	Leicestershire Regiment
Owen, P.	Royal Warwickshire Regiment
Owen, W. T.	Somerset Light Infantry
Paddy, J.	Royal Warwickshire Regiment
Page, Harry	Hants. Regiment
Page, S.	Oxfordshire and Buckinghamshire
Palmer, Frank. Sen	Royal Warwickshire Regiment
Palmer, Frank. Jun.	Royal Warwickshire Regiment
Palmer, Harry	Royal Warwickshire Regiment
Palmer, H. J.	Royal Warwickshire Regiment
Palmer, L.	Leicestershire Regiment
Palmer, Wm.	Royal Warwickshire Regiment
Parker, Horace	Gloucestershire Regiment
Parker, Joseph	Royal Warwickshire Regiment
Parker, Joseph D.	Worcestershire Regiment
Parker, Jos. Hy.	Royal Garrison Artillery
Parker, Job.	Worcestershire Regiment
Parker, Sam.	*Gloucestershire Regiment*
Parker, Thos.	Royal Engineers
Parkes, Harry	Royal Garrison Artillery

Parsons, A.	Royal Air Force
Parsons, Alfred	Leicestershire Regiment
Parsons, Bertie. E. MM	Worcestershire Regiment
Parsons, E.	Royal Army Medical Corps
Parsons, Ernest	Royal Warwickshire Regiment
Parsons, F. J.	Oxfordshire and Buckinghamshire
Parsons, J. H.	Leicestershire Regiment
Parsons, J. J.	Tank Corps
Pattison, R,	Royal Air Force
Payne, Cecil	Oxfordshire and Buckinghamshire
Payne, H.	Royal Air Force
Payne, John	Labour Corps
Peachey, T.	Royal Warwickshire Regiment
Pearce, W.	Royal Warwickshire Regiment
Pendlebury, J. C.	Royal Engineers
Penn, Harry	Royal Warwickshire Regiment
Perkins, W.	Royal Marine Light Infantry
Petty, C. J.	Worcestershire Regiment
Phillips, D. J.	Devons Regiment
Phillips, E. T.	Royal Warwickshire Regiment
Phillips, F. H.	R. B. A
Phillips, F H	Notts and Derby Regiment
Phillips, G.	Coldstream Guards
Phillips, G.	1st Life Guards
Phillips, George	Royal Warwickshire Regiment
Phillips, R. J.	Hants. Regiment
Phillips, Thomas	Royal Warwickshire Regiment
Phillips, Wilfred	HMS Griffon
Phillips, W.	HMS Carlisle
Pickard, Arthur	Royal West Kent Regiment
Pickard, Joseph	Royal Sussex Regiment
Pickard, John	Royal Warwickshire Regiment
Pickard, L.	Essex Regiment
Pickard, Sam	Royal Garrison Artillery
Pickard, S.	West Yorkshire Regiment
Pickard, R. W.	Royal Warwickshire Regiment
Picker, A.	Machine Gun Corps

Pickering, J. W.	Royal Warwickshire Regiment
Pickering, S. G.	Royal Warwickshire Regiment
Piggon, Wm. E.	Cyclist Corps
Pike, A. L.	Royal Warwickshire Regiment
Pike, C. R.	Hants. Regiment
Pike, J. L.	Machine Gun Corps
Piper, A. C.	Coldstream Guards
Pitham, J.	Royal Warwickshire Regiment
Pittam, J.	
Plackett, A.	Royal Warwickshire Regiment
Plackett, H.	Royal Field Artillery
Playle, F.	Royal Field Artillery
Playle, S.	Royal Field Artillery
Plumridge, C.	*Wiltshire Regiment*
Poole, David	Royal Warwickshire Regiment
Poole, N. C.	Royal Engineers
Pratt, A.	Royal Field Artillery
Prideaux, A. F.	Wiltshire Regiment
Prideaux, F.	Royal Field Artillery
Price, Geo. S.	Royal Warwickshire Regiment
Priest, Chas, Hy.	Cavalry Reserve
Priest, E. D.	Oxfordshire and Buckinghamshire
Priest, John	Royal Warwickshire Regiment
Priest, Sam	Royal Warwickshire Regiment
Priest, Thos.	Royal Engineers
Proctor, L.	Royal Warwickshire Regiment
Proctor, R.	Royal Warwickshire Regiment
Queensborough, Fred	Leicestershire Regiment
Radburn, A.	Somerset Light Infantry
Randall, W. R.	Royal Engineers
Randle, A. L.	King's Royal Rifle Corps
Randle, Arthur	Royal Fusiliers
Randle, C. H.	Royal Field Artillery
Randle, E.	Royal Engineers
Randle, E. W.	Royal Warwickshire Regiment
Randle, Frank	Gloucestershire Regiment
Randle, F.	Duke of Cornwall's Light Infantry

Randle, H.	*Royal Warwickshire Regiment*
Randle, Isaac. MM	Royal Field Artillery
Randle, Jack	Royal Warwickshire Regiment
Randle, Jack	Royal Air Force
Randle, John	Northants Regiment
Randle, John	R. D. C
Randle, John	Royal Engineers
Randle, John T.	Royal Warwickshire Regiment
Randle, Jos.	
Randle, Joseph H.	Royal Warwickshire Regiment
Randle, Lionel MM with bar	King's Royal Rifle Corps
Randle, N.	Royal Warwickshire Regiment
Randle, Oliver	Royal Warwickshire Regiment
Randle, P. W.	Leicestershire Regiment
Randle, S.	Royal Air Force
Randle, T.	Royal Warwickshire Regiment
Randle, Thomas	Royal Warwickshire Regiment
Randle, W. E.	
Rathbone, Fred	Somerset Light Infantry
Rawlings, Fred	Royal Army Service Corps
Rayner, F.	West Lancashire Regiment
Rayson, S	Royal Artillery
Rayson, T. H.	Leicester Regiment
Reader, E.	Royal Warwickshire Regiment
Reader, Ernest	Royal Engineers
Reader, H.	Royal Fusiliers
Reed, Henry	North Staffordshire Regiment
Reynolds, C.	Royal Warwickshire Regiment
Reynolds, Henry	Royal Warwickshire Regiment
Reynolds, J.	Royal Warwickshire Regiment
Reynolds, Percy.	Royal Warwickshire Regiment
Rice, G.	Essex Regiment
Rice, Walter.	R. N. S. B. R
Richards, A.	Machine Gun Corps
Richards, Bert.	Howe Batt
Richards, Edward	Royal Engineers
Richards, E.	Royal Warwickshire Regiment

Richards, F. G.	Royal Engineers
Richards, Jack	Machine Gun Corps
Richards, S.	Machine Gun Corps
Richards, T.	Royal Warwickshire Regiment
Richards, W.	Royal Warwickshire Regiment
Richards, William	York and Lancaster Regiment
Riley, Cecil	Lancashire Fusiliers
Riley, Ernest W.	HMS Conqueror
Riley, H. A.	Cyclist Corps
Roberts, Clifford	Royal Warwickshire Regiment
Roberts, W. F.	Royal Engineers
Robinson, E. C.	Oxfordshire and Buckinghamshire
Robinson, Frank	Coldstream Guards
Robinson, George H.	HMS City of London
Robinson, Z. A.	Coldstream Guards
Rogers, William	Royal Engineers
Ross, J. T.	Oxfordshire and Buckinghamshire
Rouse, James	Royal Warwickshire Regiment
Rowe, A.	Royal Engineers
Rowe, A.	Labour Batt.
Rowe, C. H.	Royal Engineers
Rowe, E.	Royal Army Service Corps
Rowe, F. W.	Royal Warwickshire Regiment
Rowland, S.	Royal Warwickshire Regiment
Russell, A. V.	Royal Field Artillery
Russell, J. H.	Royal Warwickshire Regiment
Russell, J. W.	Devons Regiment
Russell, W. Hugh	Grenadier Guards
Russell, Jos. Hy.	Gloucestershire Regiment
Salt, John. K.	HMS St. George
Sammons, W. H.	Res. Emp. Coy
Sandall, W.	Cyclist Battalion
Sandon, John	HMS Queen
Sandon, S.	*Oxfordshire and Buckinghamshire*
Sanders, Ernest	Royal Field Artillery
Sanders, Harry	Devons Labour Battalion
Sayers, E. J.	Royal Warwickshire Regiment

Scrimshire, P.	Royal Warwickshire Regiment
Scholes, H.	Labour Coy.
Sergeant, Thos. E.	Scottish Rifles
Sedgewick, W. A.	Royal Garrison Artillery
Sharpe, B.	Royal Warwickshire Regiment
Sharpe, F.	Royal Warwickshire Regiment
Sharpe, H.	Gloucestershire Regiment
Sharpe, H.	Royal Warwickshire Regiment
Sharpe, John. W.	Oxfordshire and Buckinghamshire
Sharpe, L.	T. R. B.
Sharpe, S.	Royal Warwickshire Regiment
Sharpe, W. A.	Royal Warwickshire Regiment
Sharrott, H.	
Sharrott, J.	Royal Field Artillery
Shaw, A.	Royal Berkshire Regiment
Shaw, J.	Royal Field Artillery
Shaw, J.	Tank Corps
Sherriff, S.	Leicester Regiment
Sherriff, T. W.	Royal Engineers
Sherwood, F.	Canadian Contigent
Sherwood, J.	Worcestershire Regiment
Shires, Samuel	Gloucestershire Regiment
Shirley, R.	*Leicester Regiment*
Shilcock, R. H.	Hampshire Regiment
Shortridge, Leon.W. DCM MM	Royal Engineers
Slater, J. E.	Royal Welsh Fusiliers
Slater, R. C.	Royal Warwickshire Regiment
Smalley, J. E.	Cam. Scottish Rifles
Smith	Royal Army Service Corps
Smith, A.	Royal Warwickshire Regiment
Smith, A. C.	Royal Engineers
Smith, C. H.	Royal Field Artiller
Smith, E.	Royal Navy Auxiliary Service
Smith, F.	Royal Field Artillery
Smith, Gilbert	Royal Garrison Artillery
Smith, Isaac	Royal Warwickshire Regiment
Smith, James	Essex Regiment

Smith, J. A.	Royal Field Artillery
Smith, J.	Northants Regiment
Smith, Samuel	Royal Warwickshire Regiment
Smith, Samuel	Royal Warwickshire Regiment
Smith, S. V.	M. T.
Smith, T. H.	Labour Corps
Smith, W.	A. F. A
Smith, W. E.	Machine Gun Corps
Smith, W. H.	Royal Welsh Fusiliers
Smith, William	Royal Engineers
Somerton, A.	Royal Field Artillery
Spencer, B.	Royal Garrison Artillery
Spencer, W.	Royal Irish Rifles
Spencer, W. J.	Royal Warwickshire Regiment
Spencer, W. T.	
Sproson, H.	Royal Warwickshire Regiment
Sproson, J. H.	Machine Gun Corps
Starkey, G. E.	Machine Gun Corps
Starkey, H.	Royal Field Artillery
Starkey, J.	
Stevens,	Royal Flying Corps
Stillgoe, Fred.	Duke of Cornwall's Light Infantry
Stokes, Edward	Worcestershire Regiment
Stokes, G. E.	
Stokes, H. Harold	Royal Warwickshire Regiment
Stokes, J.	Royal Field Artillery
Stringer, J.	Somerset Light Infantry
Suffolk, J. L.B.	HMS Marlborough
Swain, James	Royal Engineers
Swain, J. W.	Leicestershire Regiment
Swain, Sidney	Royal Navy Volunteer Reserve
Swindells, S.	Royal Warwickshire Regiment
Tallis, Abraham	Seaforth Highlanders
Tallis, Fred.	Royal Field Artillery
Tallis, J.	Royal Warwickshire Regiment
Tallis, John	Worcestershire Regiment
Tallis, R.	HMS Cleopatra

Tallis, Tom.	Labour Corps
Tallis, Thos. MM	Royal Warwickshire Regiment
Tallis, Thomas	Oxfordshire and Buckinghamshire
Tallis, T. William.	Leicestershire Regiment
Tallis, Tom	Devons Regiment
Tallis, W. A.	Highland Light Infantry
Tasker, J. A.	Royal Berkshire Regiment
Taylor, Albert	Devons Regiment
Taylor, Arthur	Royal Air Force
Taylor, Ephraim	R. N. S. B. R
Taylor, Ernest	Royal Warwickshire Regiment
Taylor, G.	Royal Warwickshire Regiment
Taylor, G.	Machine Gun Corps
Taylor, G.. S.	Honourable Artillery Company
Taylor, George.	*Royal Warwickshire Regiment*
Taylor, G.	Duke of Cornwall's Light Infantry
Taylor, Herbert	Royal Fusiliers
Taylor, J.	Machine Gun Corps
Taylor, J.	Royal Air Force
Taylor, Joseph	Royal Warwickshire Regiment
Taylor, J. T.	Royal Warwickshire Regiment
Taylor, Zadok	Royal Warwickshire Regiment
Tedds, Arthur	Royal Warwickshire Regiment
Tedds, Bert	East Surrey Regiment
Tedds, B. E.	Royal Field Artillery
Tedds, James	Royal Field Artillery
Tedds, Joseph	Royal Warwickshire Regiment
Tedds, Luther	Yorkshire Light Infantry
Tedds, W.	Royal Warwickshire Regiment
Thomas, David	Welsh Regiment
Thomas, T.	Manchester Regiment
Thorne, Daniel	Royal Engineers
Thornton, W. Mitchell	Cheshire Regiment
Thorpe, J.	Royal Warwickshire Regiment
Tidman, John	Royal Warwickshire Regiment
Tidman, Sam	King's Liverpool Regiment
Tidman, W.	Royal Warwickshire Regiment

Till, A. J.	Anti-Aircraft Artillery
Till, J. W.	Royal Sussex Regiment
Tilley, John	Royal Warwickshire Regiment
Timms, W.	Royal Berkshire Regiment
Timms, W.	Oxfordshire and Buckinghamshire
Tomlinson, Ern. M.	Royal Field Artillery
Tompkins, W.	Royal Field Artillery
Tonks, T.	Cyclist Corps
Tonks, Joseph	Royal Engineers
Topp, J. E.	R. M. E
Townsend, F.	Norfolks Regiment
Townsend, H.	Labour Corps
Townsend, H. J.	Royal Army Service Corps
Townsend, Isaac.	*Royal Warwickshire Regiment*
Townsend, W.	Tank Corps
Trafford, E.	Devons Regiment
Tranter, A.	Machine Gun Corps
Treadwell, G.	Coldstream Guards
Treadwell, J.	Royal Warwickshire Regiment
Treadwell, M.	Coldstream Guards
Trim, J. D.	Royal Engineers
Tudge, G. W. A.	Royal Field Artillery
Turner, F. J.	*Oxfordshire and Buckinghamshire*
Turner, George	R. M. L. I., HMS Hussar
Turner, J. R.	West Kent Regiment
Turner, W. L.	Oxfordshire and Buckinghamshire
Twigger	M. G. L.
Twigger	Royal Engineers
Twigger, A.	Labour Corps
Twigger, A.	Worcestershire Regiment
Twigger, A. E.	Tank Corps
Twigger, Bert.	Coldstream Guards
Twigger, G.	M. G. Guards
Twigger, George	M. G. Sec. Gds. Brigade
Twigger, Harry	Coldstream Guards
Twigger, J.	Yorkshire and Lancaster Regiment
Twigger, J.	Army Service Corps

Twigger, J. T.	Royal Warwickshire Regiment
Twigger, Sam	Machine Gun Corps
Twigger, T.	R. S. D.
Twigger, T.	Royal Army Service Corps
Twigger, Wm.	Royal Warwickshire Regiment
Tyler, E.	Royal Air Force
Tyler, H.	Royal Garrison Artillery
Varney, William	Worcestershire Regiment
Vaughan, A. Thos.	Royal Berkshire Regiment
Wagstaff, George M.	Lancashire Fusiliers
Wagstaff, G.	Oxfordshire and Buckinghamshire
Walker, A.	Royal Navy
Walker, A. E.	*Oxfordshire and Buckinghamshire*
Walker, F. F.	Royal Warwickshire Regiment
Walker, Ar. J.	Royal Irish Regiment
Walker, A. J.	Oxfordshire and Buckinghamshire
Walker, J.	R. M. A
Walker, Jack MM	Royal Warwickshire Regiment
Walker, T. W.	Worcestershire Regiment
Walton, G. Haydon.	*Royal Warwickshire Regiment*
Wanless, J.	Connaught Rangers
Ward, A.	Royal Warwickshire Regiment
Ward, Chas.	Royal Warwickshire Regiment
Ward, H.	King's Royal Rifle Corps
Warner, W. D.	Royal Garrison Artillery
Warner, W. J.	Royal Army Service Corps
Warren, Arthur	Oxfordshire and Buckinghamshire
Waterfield	Royal Army Service Corps
Webb, Alick	Royal Sussex Regiment
Webb, Arthur	Royal Field Artillery
Webb, J. T.	Royal Field Artillery
Webb, T. V.	Royal Marine Light Infantry
Webb, Tom	Royal Field Artillery
Webb, W.	Royal Garrison Artillery
Wells, H. G.	Kings Royal Rifle Corps
West, J. T.	Royal Field Artillery
Wetton, Thomas	Royal Warwickshire Regiment

Wheatley, C. B.	Royal Warwickshire Regiment
Wheatley, Thomas	Royal Field Artillery
Whelan MM	Irish Fusiliers
Whitcroft, S.	Machine Gun Corps
Whitcroft, W.	Royal Warwickshire Regiment
White, A.	Royal Warwickshire Regiment
White, Bert	Hants Regiment
White, Fred	Leicestershire Regiment
White, H.	Cyclist Battalion
White, W. E.	Sherwood Rangers
Whitehall, A.	St. John's Ambulance
Whitehall, E.	St. John's Ambulance
Whitehead, D. F.	Army Ordnance Corps
Whitehead, J. F.	Royal Scots
Whitehead, J.	Royal Warwickshire Regiment
Whitehead, J. F.	Royal Field Artillery
Whitehead, John	Cyclist Corps
Whitehead, Thomas	Royal Warwickshire Regiment
Whitehead, Jos. H.	Oxfordshire and Buckinghamshire
Whitehead, William	Machine Gun Corps
Whitehouse, Isaac	Royal Field Artillery
Whyman, J. MM	Royal Warwickshire Regiment
Wight, H.	Royal Warwickshire Regiment
Wilcox, E.	Royal Engineers
Wilcox, F. C.	Machine Gun Corps
Wild, A. J.	Royal Berkshire Regiment
Wild, C. W.	Machine Gun Corps
Wilkes, Samuel	South Staffordshire Regiment
Wilkes, Hy. T.	Royal Warwickshire Regiment
Willet, G. C.	Bucks
Willett, J. A.	Leicestershire Regiment
Williams, Isaac	Northants Regiment
Williams, John	R.N.S. B. R
Williams, James	South Staffordshire Regiment
Williams, J. H.	Royal Sussex Regiment
Wilkinson, J. H.	
Wilkinson, J. H.	Berkshire Yeomanry

Wills, T. W.	Royal Marine Light Infantry
Willshee, A. T.	Devons Cyclist
Willshee, T.	Royal Warwickshire Regiment
Willis, John T.	
Willis, Wm. J.	
Wilson, John	Royal Warwickshire Regiment
Wilson, John	Dorsets Regiment
Witts, H.	Coldstream Guards
Wood, D.	Royal Warwickshire Regiment
Wood, J.	Royal Engineers
Woodward, Hubert Reginald	Australian Infantry
Worthington, Tom	Royal Artillery
Wright, H.	Royal Field Artillery (Anti-Aircraft)
Wright, H.	Northamptonshire Regiment
Wright, Frank	Royal Field Artillery
Wright, J.	Royal Horse Artillery
Wright, Edward	Northants Regiment
Wright, J.	Royal Warwickshire Regiment
Wright, R.	Royal Field Artillery
Wright, W. G.	Royal Warwickshire Regiment
Wright, E. V.	Oxfordshire and Buckinghamshire
Wright, E. V.	Royal Munster Fusiliers
Wrighting, H. C.	King's African Rifles
Wyatt, Fred. H.	Wiltshire Regiment
Wyatt, J. S.	Norfolk Regiment
Wyatt, T.	South Lancashire Regiment
Wyatt, T.	M. M. P.
Yardley, J. G.	Royal Fusiliers
Young, A. E.	Royal Marines
Young, P.	Rifle Brigade

Women's Auxiliary Army Corps

Armitage, Elsie	WRAF
Amos, Winifred Annie	WRAF
Lovett, Millicent	QMAAC
Preston, Maud	QMAAC

Index